SHOTGUN JUSTICE

ONE PROSECUTOR'S
CRUSADE AGAINST
CRIME AND CORRUPTION IN
ALEXANDRIA & ARLINGTON

MICHAEL LEE POPE

Charleston   London

THE
History
PRESS

Published by The History Press
Charleston, SC 29403
www.historypress.net

Copyright © 2012 by Michael Lee Pope
All rights reserved

Cover image: Crandal Mackey, 1905. *Courtesy of the Virginia Room, Arlington Public Library.*

First published 2012

Manufactured in the United States

ISBN 978.1.60949.747.7

Library of Congress CIP data applied for.

To Shooter Pope
1941–2012

CONTENTS

ACKNOWLEDGEMENTS

My lovely wife, Hope Nelson, whose eagle eye and endless patience made this book happen.

My mother, Diana Pope, without whom none of this would be possible.

Brandy Crist-Travers, whose talent helped capture a forgotten era.

George Combs, who helped me track down the obscure and the profane.

ARLINGTON CONFIDENTIAL

P*sst*! Here's a story that's confidential. In fact it's so secretive that almost nobody knows about the hidden history of Rosslyn, where bodies were dumped in Dead Man's Hollow. It's so arcane that nobody has ever heard of Jackson City, a place so awful people called it "Hell's Bottom." And don't start asking people in Del Ray about the St. Asaph Racetrack because it's long gone and totally forgotten. Until now.

The legend of Crandal Mackey has been lost to time, a forgotten relic of an era when political corruption was rampant and crime was violent. Even the name of the jurisdiction has faded away as Alexandria County became Arlington County. People walk through Crandal Mackey Park today and have no idea about the dangerous roadhouses that once populated the intersection. Visitors to the Arlington County sheriff's office have probably seen the shotgun mounted on the wall but never asked why it was there or who once wielded it. But it's an important story because it shaped the contours of modern life in Arlington County, where skyscrapers now dominate the landscape. The events of Mackey's time in office also played a central role in the creation of the Del Ray neighborhood in Alexandria.

One place where the legacy of Crandal Mackey is evident is the Virginia Room at Arlington Central Library. Here is where visitors can see a striking watercolor painting by Rudy Wendelin, an artist best known for his depiction of Smokey the Bear. In the late 1970s, he was commissioned to create a portrait of Mackey in action by Arlington civic activist Marianne Karydes. She was working with the League of Women Voters to create a program for

This watercolor painting by artist Rudy Wendelin captures the chaos of a raid, complete with the posse destroying slot machines and tearing down paintings. *Virginia Room, Arlington Public Library.*

high school students, and she was seeking a way to vividly portray an era before color photography.

"Bless you for coming through, again, as you always do," she wrote in a letter to Wendelin.

The letter to Wendelin is a blueprint for a Hollywood movie, setting the scene for an epic conflict between corrupt gamblers and a crusading prosecutor. Karydes explained that Mackey led a posse armed with sledgehammers, axes and at least one sawed-off shotgun. The "good guys" called themselves the Good Citizens League and boarded a train in Washington headed for the seedy side of the Potomac.

When they arrived at Jackson City, Karydes explained to Wendelin, they entered a two-story clapboard saloon and wreaked havoc—"something like you would see in an old Western set." A jukebox playing "There'll Be a Hot Time in the Old Town Tonight" was knocked over but continued to play. Tables were knocked over. Liquor bottles were broken. Fists were flying along with axes and sledgehammers. The good guys were in vests and suits, while the bad guys were in shirtsleeves with no collar and garters on their sleeves. They had "villainous mustaches" and striped shirts.

"Crandal Mackey had a black mustache (not handlebar, just brush) and wore a derby," Karydes explained. "Generally handsome man, long, slightly thin face."

It was a violent scene, exposing the clash between good and evil. But it may have been sanitized just a bit.

"We better omit the scarlet ladies," Karydes suggested. "This is going to be shown to school kids!"

Mackey was an iconoclast, a reformer and an outcast. He won election as the commonwealth's attorney for Alexandria County in 1903 with a two-vote margin of victory. That's a difficult mandate for any elected official, especially one who wanted to overturn the machine that ran Virginia at the dawn of the twentieth century. Instead of second-guessing himself, though, Mackey grabbed his shotgun and conducted a series of raids with a posse of men carrying axes and shovels.

It wasn't an easy fight. Gambling had deep roots in history of Virginia and the psychology of Alexandria. The money to finance the colony of Virginia came from a game of chance, a lottery approved by King James I in 1612. George Washington himself bought and sold lottery tickets, including snatching up the first ticket for the first federal lottery in 1793. The public wharves on the waterfront in Alexandria were built using revenue from lottery tickets.

Not only did Crandal Mackey have to work against that deep-seated human impulse to gamble, but he also had to take on some of the highest and lowest men of his era. He faced down two-bit gamblers. He closed saloons. He got into fistfights with railroad lawyers. And he fought the machine. In the end, his own party turned against him. It wasn't quite a rejection of what he had accomplished, although even today we can hear echoes that the reform movement was just some kind of misguided adventure.

"After the war, do-gooders forced the reluctant police to raid and close down the public gambling houses," observed Alexandria historian Frederick Tilp.

Clearly, Tilp had Mackey in mind when he wrote those words. Others view the Mackey legacy in more flattering terms.

"Arlingtonians owe a great debt of gratitude to Crandal Mackey and his group of civic crusaders," concluded Arlington historian Eleanor Lee Templeman.

In the end, Mackey's record is somewhat mixed. He shut down the violet dens in Rosslyn and wiped Jackson City off the map forever, but he also let the corrupt politicians walk as long as they closed their gambling operations and went about their business as if nothing had happened. Nothing to see

Crandal Mackey stands in front of the Sorrell Sunday bar, a notorious spot in Hell's Bottom. *Virginia Room, Arlington Public Library.*

here, folks. Perhaps that's why enemies in his own party ended up taking him out in the end.

Nobody really knows why Crandal Mackey mysteriously abandoned his campaign for reelection in 1915. Was it because he was threatened? Newspapers from the era were full of stories about the prosecutor and his family receiving regular threats of violence. Did they shut him down? Was Commonwealth's Attorney Crandal Mackey silenced? Unfortunately, no one is alive today who can answer that question. The heavy hand of time has obscured the true crime story about this crusading prosecutor and the shotgun that he wielded with a sense of frontier justice.

Again and again, lawyers representing some of the most powerful forces in Virginia politics went after the commonwealth's attorney from Alexandria County. They tried to delay. They tried to obfuscate. They tried to bribe. They tried violence and politics, sometimes at the same time.

"Elections in those days resulted in opponents labeling each other with rather pointed nicknames and sometimes using gunfire," wrote Templeman. "In one election the defeated candidate for sheriff announced that he was

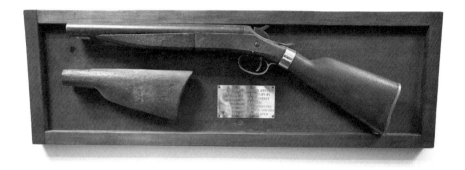

Crandal Mackey's shotgun is on display in the office of the Arlington County sheriff. *Brandy Crist-Travers.*

going out to kill Mackey, whom he felt had worked against him. With calm courage, Mackey ignored the threat."

Crandal Mackey believed in this sort of shotgun justice. Back-alley gamblers were as much at risk as elected officials on the take. Just as the tortoise slowly worked toward his goals in Aesop's fable, here was a man who was willing to wait for the fickle finger of fate.

The Rise of Crandal Mackey

Crandal Mackey was born in a Confederate ambulance in Shreveport, Louisiana, eight months after the end of the Civil War. The date was December 15, 1865, a time when the South was just beginning a long, slow climb back to civilization. The Union left the region in shambles and destroyed, its resources damaged and its economy in tatters. And yet even though the South was defeated on the battlefield, the spirit of the South was undefeated.

President Andrew Johnson had just restored habeas corpus, which had been suspended during the war. Northern congressmen sought to exact punishment on Southern states, forming committees on Reconstruction to guide the difficult process of readmitting rebellious Southern states. Nine days after Mackey's birth, the Ku Klux Klan was formed in Tennessee as a secret society to terrorize blacks.

Before the war, the Mackeys lived in Washington, D.C. The 1860 census places the family in the house of Richard Lloyd, a forty-seven-year-old lawyer who lived in Ward 3 of the city. The document shows fourteen people living in the household, including twenty-eight-year-old Richard Mackey and his wife, Rosina Mackey, along with their two-year-old son, Lloyd Mackey. Lloyd must have been one of the leading attorneys of the era, because his real estate holdings are listed at $30,000. His personal estate is listed as $10,000, and his household includes two servants.

The Mackey family had long roots in America, arriving in Jefferson County, Georgia, in the 1700s. Crandal Mackey's great-grandfather was

James Mackey, a Revolutionary War hero who served as a sergeant in the Sixth South Carolina. On February 28, 1776, he was mustered into the South Carolina state troops. During the war, the regiment saw action in South Carolina, Florida and Georgia. The 1790 census shows James Mackey living in Charleston and owning twenty-six slaves.

His son, John Mackey, grew up in Waxhaw, South Carolina, with Andrew Jackson. John Mackey later served with the man who would later be known as "Old Hickory" in the Revolutionary War as part of an independent company of South Carolina troops commended by his uncle, Charles Mackey. As a sixteen-year-old solider, John Mackey corralled horses and was captured by the British at Camden. The enemy eventually confined him at Charleston.

After the war, he is listed in a Charleston directory a "goaler," which meant he was a prison officer or jailer of some sort. By 1820, he is listed as the head of a household with five whites and five slaves. In 1822, he married Mary Mills Dulaney and began having children. One of those children was Thomas Jefferson Mackey, who was born in 1830. Thomas Jefferson Mackey graduated from the Citadel Academy in Charleston and then headed off to law school at Harvard. By the time he turned thirty in 1860, according to census records, he was already a successful lawyer in South Carolina.

When war broke out with Mexico, Thomas Jefferson Mackey dropped his burgeoning legal career, enlisted with the Palmetto Regiment of the South Carolina volunteers and headed to the front lines of battle. The Mexican-American War has been largely forgotten these days, but it served as a prelude to the Civil War in many ways. The Mexicans had been independent of Spain for only a few years before General Zachary Taylor invaded the Rio Grande. The lust for Manifest Destiny was so blinding that few had foresight to see what would happen once the vast land acquisition upset the delicate balance of slave states and free states.

Thomas Jefferson Mackey found himself in one of the climactic battles of General Winfield Scott's push to Mexico City, the Battle of Churubusco. Mackey was severely wounded while storming the heights of Chapultepec, and his obituary noted that he "never fully recovered" from the injury. As a result, he spent the rest of the war as a private secretary to Robert Kingston Scott, who would later become the first governor of a readmitted South Carolina after the Civil War.

When the South left the Union, Mackey enlisted in the Confederate army and was appointed a captain of engineers, serving on the staff of General Sterling Price throughout the war. When Union General William Tecumseh Sherman burned and looted his way across the South, the Mackey family ended up in Shreveport, Louisiana. There, on December 15, 1865, Crandal Mackey was born in the back of a Confederate ambulance.

The Mackeys had five children: Lloyd in 1860, Beckford in 1865, Crandal also in 1865, Argyle in 1868 and Thomas Jefferson Mackey Jr. in 1870. Census records show that Beckford went off to a religious boarding school and ended up practicing law in Mexico. Argyle enrolled in a Baltimore medical school, and Thomas Jefferson Mackey Jr. entered the insurance business in Washington, D.C.

Crandal Mackey followed in his father's footsteps. The law was to become Crandal Mackey's life, carrying on a family tradition that was well known in the South Carolina bar associations. But living up to the legacy of Thomas Jefferson Mackey must have been a difficult chore. In addition to being a war hero and respected judge, the father was also the noted author of "Life of R.E. Lee" and "Life of George Washington."

The 1870 census lists Thomas Jefferson Mackey as a trial justice in Ward 1 of Charleston, and the 1880 census lists him as a circuit judge in District 35, just south of the border from Charlotte, North Carolina. There, in a little town called Chester, young Crandal Mackey worked the cotton fields when he wasn't engaged in studies. When he was a teenager, he attended South Carolina Military Institute and became part of the Centennial Battalion. Crandal Mackey then enrolled at Randolph Macon College in Ashland, Virginia, where he enjoyed boxing and football. He graduated from Carolina Military Institute in Charlotte, North Carolina, before returning to South Carolina.

But the Palmetto State did not suit him. Or perhaps he did not want to live under the long shadow of his father. Whatever the reason, Crandal Mackey moved to Washington, D.C., in 1885 and took a job at the War Department while studying law at Georgetown University. He graduated from law school in 1889 and became an active part of the legal community.

Newspapers of the era are full of legal notices documenting young Crandal Mackey's career, which began representing clients in real estate transactions in the District of Columbia. At one point, he left the legal field to become a pension examiner and land speculator. In 1897, Mackey moved to Virginia and erected a home at 1711 Twenty-second Street North—a house known as Rock Hill. He built on two acres purchased from his mother, who had inherited a large tract from her father.

After scoring a number of deals in the Trinidad neighborhood, Crandal Mackey heard the drums of war. As was the case with his father before him and a generation before, Crandal Mackey took up arms against the enemy.

Crandal Mackey had five sons and two daughters. *Virginia Room, Arlington Public Library.*

This time, it was Spain. So Mackey enlisted in the army, and President William McKinley appointed him captain of the Tenth United States Immunes in Richmond.

As captain of the company, Mackey was responsible for 103 men on his roll, 3 more than the minimum requirement. Soon, he left Richmond on the way to Augusta, Georgia, where his regiment was scheduled to rendezvous. Like the Mexican-American War that his father fought, the Spanish-American War has been largely forgotten. Perhaps this is due to the respective aims of the wars—Thomas Jefferson Mackey fought for Manifest Destiny and Crandal Mackey for colonialism.

In some ways, the Spanish-American War would be a turning point for Crandal Mackey, who was thirty-three at the time. It was the first time he accomplished something major for himself outside the orbit of his father. It was the first time he saw the horrors of war, an experience that undoubtedly shaped his instincts in the courtroom. And, perhaps most importantly, it was when he became known as "Captain." Throughout his career, friends and enemies would refer to Captain Mackey.

After the Spanish-American War, Crandal Mackey returned to his legal practice in Washington, D.C. It didn't take long for Captain Mackey to form

During the Spanish-American War, Crandal Mackey served as a captain. *Virginia Room, Arlington Public Library.*

an interest in politics. The first official record of Mackey's involvement in public life is September 1900, just before the election that year. Mackey is listed along with Frank Lyon as vice-president of the Bryan, Stevenson and Rixey Club. The Democratic slate that year included failed presidential candidate William Jennings Bryan, former Vice President Adlai Stevenson Sr. (Bryan's vice presidential choice) and incumbent Congressman John Rixey, who would be the only successful candidate of the three. The next spring, Crandal Mackey was listed as a speaker at a mass meeting for the Democratic state convention campaign at the Carne schoolhouse.

This was a time when a new sense of Southern Progressivism was taking hold in Virginia, although the commonwealth's version of the movement wasn't about exposing the ills of tenement housing or meat inspections. This reform effort was aimed squarely at preventing African Americans from voting, a goal that was seen at the time as "good government," a "progressive" initiative, because the black vote was seen as a corrupting influence. In later years, this interpretation was unveiled as a twisted fantasy.

"In part, disfranchisement was also presented as a progressive reform, the sure means of purging Southern elections of the corruption that disgraced them," wrote historian C. Vann Woodward. "In no mood for paradoxes, Southerners generally accepted Negro disfranchisement as a reform, without taking second thought."

The standard device, used across the New South, was to set up a series of barriers such as property requirements or literacy qualifications. Loopholes were created just large enough to let bumbling white illiterates through, of course, sometimes known as a "grandfather clause" or, perhaps more perniciously, "good character clause." The effort swept through the South like a wildfire—South Carolina in 1895, Louisiana in 1898, North Carolina in 1900, Alabama in 1901 and Virginia in 1902. Again and again, the disenfranchisement of blacks was sold as a progressive reform to prevent corruption of politics.

"The blind spot in the Southern progressive record—as, for that matter, in the national movement—was the Negro, for the whole movement in the South coincided paradoxically with the crest of the wave of racism," Woodward explained. "The typical progressive reformer rode to power in the South on a disfranchising or white supremacy movement."

Republicans used black votes to maintain power during Reconstruction, a time that's still viewed with bitterness and skepticism. The Union had suspended habeas corpus to win the war. After it was over, they used the power of the federal government to have their way in the commonwealth. But the war left Virginia in a depression with crushing debt and few choices. Even before the war began, leaders in Richmond were piling on debt for railroads and canals. When the smoke cleared, the commonwealth had interrupted payments on a $45 million debt and had no way to dig out of the hole. Just paying the interest on the debt was $2.7 million per year.

"After the war, virtually every Virginian was cash poor," wrote historian Peter Wallenstein. "When evaluating the operations of their state government, residents found taxes high but benefits scant."

This was a time when a group of Democrats known as the Funders emerged in state politics, urging that the public debt be paid in full. The Funders believed that this was even more important than public education, so they diverted money from schools to pay down the debt. Unlike in other states, where Republicans could be blamed for high postwar taxes and mounting public debt, Democrats had controlled the General Assembly ever since the end of the war. This meant that there wasn't an opportunity for the kind of white vigilante violence perpetrated by the Ku Klux Klan to reduce

The Mackey home, known as Rock Hill, was at 1711 North Twenty-second Street, near Dead Man's Hollow. *Virginia Room, Arlington Public Library.*

the black electorate. But the struggle for power in Virginia moved with the changing season, and the winds of change were blowing in Richmond.

The Funders set the state for the Readjusters, a biracial and bipartisan alliance that took control of the House of Delegates and Virginia state Senate in the election of 1879. Instead of paying the debt in full, which seemed like an impossible task, the Readjusters hope to partially repudiate the debt and make a good-faith effort to pay the balance. But with the Funders controlling the Governor's Mansion, the two sides clashed repeatedly, leading into the bare-knuckled election of 1881. The *Richmond Dispatch* handicapped the race this way: "There's Cameron, he's for the Democrats; and there's Lewis, he's for the negroes; and there's Blair, he's for the Greenback lunatics." William Evelyn Cameron won the election, and the Readjusters had total control of Virginia politics.

"For a short time, the negro seemed about to become a part of the political people," wrote historian Charles Pearson. "But the habit of implicit obedience to overseers and a boss proved too strong."

Although the Readjusters were able to make substantial contributions to African American schools, their attempts to regulate the railroads were

Thomas Staples Martin was a railroad lawyer from Scottsville who built a powerful political machine in Virginia after Reconstruction. *Library of Congress.*

unsuccessful. And even though their attempts to draw capital from other states worked to stimulate the economy, the conspicuous presence of blacks at the upper reaches of the government provoked a white backlash. By the end of Governor Cameron's term in 1885, warring factions within the Readjuster Party allowed Democrat Fitzhugh Lee to win a lopsided victory.

"I thank God that the white wings of the angel of peace have spread over this land," Lee exclaimed at a rally in Richmond on the eve of his election. "I am one of those who rejoice that the sword has been beaten into a ploughshare and the sabre into a pruning hook, and that the reign of peace, unity, and fraternity shall be as ever lasting as the home of the stars, as eternal as the foundations of the everlasting hills."

Just in case the crowd didn't get it, the band struck up "Dixie" at the end of his speech, and the crowd yelled until it was hoarse. Lee's victory marked the beginning of Democratic Party domination that would last for more than three-quarters of a century. The following year, railroad executive John Warwick Daniel replaced Readjuster Party boss William Mahone. A few years later, Daniel would be joined in the United States Senate by his principal lieutenant, a young railroad executive from Scottsville named Thomas Staples Martin.

Working together, Daniel and Martin created a political machine so powerful that it ruled Virginia for decades. Their coalition was held together with finesse and flexibility, an organization that was more about power than reform. Eventually, Martin rose to power, and the organization became the Martin machine. There were challenges from populists and progressives, of course. And the Martin machine did not always get its way in Richmond or in Washington, D.C. But the organization learned to tolerate voices inside the Democratic Party it could not silence. He also built a team of supporters and sycophants who took control of the Democratic Party from the old guard Confederate heroes, a generation of businessmen and lawyers and railroad magnates.

"Martin was neither a farmer nor an aristocrat, but a shrewd railroad lawyer," wrote Virginia historian Harvie Wilkinson.

At the dawn of the twentieth century, Virginia was a cacophony of voices singing out of tune. A series of hard-fought political campaigns had been expensive, violent and corrupt. Some wanted to streamline the judicial system. Others agitated for progressive reform such as primary elections to nominate candidates for the United States Senate. Perhaps most significantly, Democratic Party leaders from the East and South wanted to deny the vote to blacks, whose allegiance to the Republican Party posed a threat.

The Martin machine knew that the only way to consolidate power was to silence the opposition, or at least rig the system to its own advantage. So, leaders in the General Assembly called for a convention to revise the reviled Underwood Constitution, the infamous Reconstruction-era document that established universal manhood suffrage and established a statewide system of publically supported schools. Voters in Virginia were eager to rid themselves of this albatross, approving the call in a spring 1900 referendum. They elected eighty-eight Democrats and twelve Republicans to a convention that met from the summer of 1901 to the summer of 1902.

As delegates gathered in Richmond for a Constitutional Convention, the goal was to figure out a way to disenfranchise blacks without running afoul of the Fourteenth Amendment. Leading the effort was Virginia Senator Carter Glass of Lynchburg, who proclaimed that his suffrage plan would "eliminate the darkey as a political factor in this State in less than five years, so that in no single county of the Commonwealth will there be the least concern felt for the complete supremacy of the white race in the affairs of government."

When one of his fellow delegates challenged the senator, asking if he intended to use fraud or discrimination, Glass was clear. "Discrimination! Why that is exactly what we propose," Glass explained. "That, exactly, is what this convention was elected for—to discriminate to the very extremity of permissible action under the limitations of the federal Constitution, with the view to the elimination of every negro voter who can be gotten rid of, legally, without materially impairing the numerical strength of the white electorate."

As historian W.J. Cash explained in his 1941 masterpiece *Mind of the South*, the era was ruled by the specter of "Progress," a word he insisted on capitalizing to show its significance. Capitalism was at the center of his critique, which claimed that the aristocratic ideal of the Old South was yielding to the lure of commerce and industry. In a chapter titled "Easing Tensions and Quiet Years," Cash claimed that money had become the *sine qua non* of social position.

"Money, in fact, was certainly the final arbiter of rank in the South now as in Detroit or San Francisco," Cash wrote. "Without it, it would take a very great name indeed to hold on to its quondam place in the sun."

This was the setting for Crandal Mackey entering the world of politics, as he did in the summer of 1901. Arriving that August in Norfolk for the gubernatorial convention, Mackey found himself in a political environment where the populists and the progressives were up against a machine bent on power. For now, at least, the odds were not as lopsided as they would become in later years. The delegates were calculated using a formula based on the number of votes cast for William Jennings Bryan in 1900. That added up to 1,441 delegates at the convention, one of the largest gatherings ever held in Virginia. Mackey was a delegate from the Washington District delegate of Alexandria County.

By August, Norfolk was sweltering with heat and politics. The executive committee of the party concluded that Norfolk was the only city in Virginia that could accommodate the scale of such an event, and people from the far reaches of the state boarded railroad cars. Even then, Norfolk might not have been able to handle such a crowd. The *Alexandria Gazette* correspondent reported that hotels were so crowded that the proprietors told delegates to go to city boardinghouses or other nearby towns for accommodations.

"There were many new faces in convention, indeed a majority of the delegates being young and new men," reported the *Gazette* correspondent.

Welcome to the Machine

As Crandal Mackey arrived on the train to Norfolk that hot and humid August 1901, a sense of electricity was in the air. The summer winds of change were blowing in Virginia, and Mackey was one of a handful of progressive new faces hoping to wrest control of the Democratic Party from the Martin machine. As the delegates streamed out of the train station and fanned out into the hotels, there was a sense that a changing of the guards was about to happen.

Both rival factions checked in to the Monticello Hotel. Located directly across the street from the Armory, where the convention was taking place, the hotel lobby became an intense scene of jockeying for position and pulling together coalitions. Conservatives were in rooms 102 and 104, while progressives were in rooms 5, 7 and 9.

Conservative Democrats supported Congressman Claude Swanson, a lawyer from Danville who was aligned with the Martin machine. Leading the forces of opposition was Attorney General Andrew Jackson Montague, an attorney from Danville who had spent the year building a massive coalition in opposition to the machine. The politics began in the immediate aftermath of the election of 1900, when Virginia cast twelve electoral votes for the unsuccessful Democratic candidate William Jennings Bryan.

Montague spent years setting the stage for this moment, beginning with his support of the Grover Cleveland presidential campaign in 1892. Cleveland won Virginia, and Montague was appointed United States attorney for the Western District of Virginia. In 1898, he was elected attorney general and

During the Democratic Convention of 1902, opposing candidates and their supporters all stayed at the Monticello Hotel. *Library of Congress.*

began building a campaign for governor. On the campaign trail, Montague charged that Senator Thomas Staples Martin was an autocrat and appealed to voters to rise up against the machine.

Swanson denied being aligned with Martin and rejected the idea any machine existed in the commonwealth. If there was a machine, Swanson said, Montague was using it. In a brazen counterattack, Swanson also charged that the first office Montague ever held was handed to him on a local machine slate.

"If you don't want Martin to hit you, don't hit Martin. And if he does hit you back, don't play the crybaby," Swanson said during a debate in Mecklenburg County, prompting a round of laughter. "If you can point me to one single corrupt act in the life of Senator Martin, I will help you fight him."

At first, it looked as though the Martin machine would be able to carry the day for Congressman Swanson. But as the months wore on, it became more and more evident that the progressives would be able to mount a serious challenge. Alexandria City Hall was the leading source of support for Swanson, and city leaders were able to keep the congressman in the lead among committed delegates in the early days of the campaign. But out in Alexandria County, Crandal Mackey was building support for the fiery attorney general. In May,

Claude Swanson was a lawyer from Danville aligned with the Martin machine. *Library of Congress.*

support from Washington County and the city of Danville were enough to put him over the edge. By the time delegates arrived in Norfolk, it was clear that Montague had the votes to upset the powerful Martin machine.

"One mistake was made early in the fight by Mr. Swanson and his friends and that was their failure to place a proper estimate upon the splendid strength of the Attorney General, either before the people of the State or as a political organizer," the *Richmond Dispatch* observed. "Mr. Montague made a brilliant stump canvass and the people flocked to hear him as though he had been the beloved 'Old Red Fox' come back from the tomb."

The moniker was a subtle nod to Montague's red hair and aggressive temperament, which were powerful assets on the campaign trail. Supporters wore white silk badges bearing a likeness of the Old Red Fox and obviously had a big time supporting their candidate. Swanson supporters complained

Andrew Jackson Montague was a lawyer from Danville who was aligned against the Martin machine. *Library of Congress.*

to the *Alexandria Gazette* that the progressives "were at times disposed to exult over those of the party who had made a gallant but unsuccessful canvass."

Swanson's team held out hope that the power of the machine might be enough to overcome the massive progressive coalition. The delegation from Warren County, for example, was split because the faction advocating Swanson was "at this time in control of the county machinery," according to the *Richmond Dispatch*. Swanson supporters complained that the Montague forces were overly exuberant in their celebration, charging that they had overcome the power of "the ring."

Across the street from the Monticello Hotel, at the Armory, electric lights filled the night air with illumination, and the electric fans took some of the sting out of the thick August humidity. This was Montague's moment to shine, but it was also an opportunity for Crandal Mackey to position himself as a rising star. By aligning himself with Montague, Mackey burst into Virginia politics as part of a fresh new generation of trailblazing progressives. The air crackled with excitement.

"The hotel lobbies are thronged with delegates and enthusiastic spectators, who are shouting for their respective favorites," the *Richmond Times* reported.

For Mackey, the election of 1901 was an opportunity to take sides in the ongoing war for control of Virginia. Casting his lot with the progressives, the young lawyer began making a name for himself in Northern Virginia as someone who would stand up to the Martin machine. It was a risky move because powerful forces of gambling interests and railroad power were lined up behind Martin and Swanson. If Swanson had been successful, Mackey's political career may have been over. But the gamble paid off.

"There was a great shake-up of the State Committee," reported the *Richmond Times* after Montague was nominated by acclamation. "Those who have been supporters of Mr. Montague are now in full control of the State machinery of the party."

It was a solid victory, paving the way for November because Virginia was essentially a one-party state in those days. The progressive attorney general had no trouble crushing Republican Hampton Hogue in November 1901, becoming the first governor of Virginia since the Civil War who had not served the Confederacy. The *Richmond Dispatch* declared that the election of 1901 "has been one of the most remarkable ever fought in the State, and has resulted in a revolution that has thrown old party leaders aside and has placed new men at the helm of Democracy."

Shortly after his inauguration, the tone of Virginia politics began to transform. One of the first items on the agenda was creation of a new constitution, one that enacted poll taxes and literacy tests to disenfranchise blacks. Ironically, this is a reform that would have been considered progressive at the time because of the common view that black votes were for sale and, therefore, a sign of corruption. Governor Montague and his progressive reformers couldn't have known it at the time, but that was a change that would undercut their success. The smaller electorate created by the 1902 constitution made it easier for the Martin machine to control the vote.

That was not yet evident in 1902, as sweeping changes began taking place in Virginia politics. After more than a year of deliberation, delegates to the Virginia Constitutional Convention were almost ready to conclude their business and adopted a new constitution. This one would be infamous for installing the rule of Jim Crow in Virginia, disenfranchising the black vote throughout the commonwealth by instituting a poll tax. It also expanded the number of state offices filled by popular election and created regulation against the wishes of the increasingly powerful railroad lobby.

"We recognize that these great powers of transportation are, like fire and water, most excellent servants, but the most destructive and unreasonable

This cartoon shows the suspicion that many whites had for blacks, who were viewed as a corrupting influence in Virginia politics. *Library of Congress.*

masters," declared constitutional convention delegate Allen Caperton Braxton of Staunton.

While Virginia Senator Carter Glass of Lynchburg was leading the charge for limiting the pool of voters during the two-year constitutional convention, Braxton and others were leading the charge for increased regulation of powerful railroad industry. The effort would result in replacing the old Board of Public Works with the much more energetic State Corporation Commission, which would swiftly go about the business of doubling the tax revenue. During one rather emotional appeal to the convention, Braxton charged that the convention needed to decide whether "the people or the railroads would control the government of the commonwealth."

In the end, the infamous constitution of 1902 created a system of tax valuation, rate regulation, employer liability and eminent domain. But all of that would be overshadowed by its most lasting legacy: the disenfranchisement of blacks. As delegates left Richmond, constitution in hand, progressivism was spreading through the South with its own distinct flavor. It was not the progressivism of Theodore Roosevelt in New York or Hiram Johnson in

California. It wasn't even the progressivism of Robert Lafollette in Wisconsin or Gifford Pinchot in Pennsylvania.

"The Progressive movement of the early twentieth century was a national phenomenon," wrote Peter Wallenstein. "Everywhere it had multiple strands, including social welfare and social control, as well as political democratization and its antitheses. In the South, because racial segregation and black disfranchisement were central to the enterprise, the two faces of progressivism were more different than elsewhere."

That created the perfect stage for Crandal Mackey to enter the scene. Newspapers of the era reflect how Mackey was making a name for himself as a reform-minded lawyer, taking labor rights cases such as that of an ironworker who died because of improper working conditions—a pulley rope broke and an iron beam fell on him during construction of the Government Printing Office. Mackey sued the builders and contractors on behalf of his estate and won $12,500 for his family.

Then he brought a case on behalf of a Southern Railway Company employee after the man suffered from frostbite while shoveling snow in Prince William County. Unfortunately for Mackey, the jury in that case returned a verdict for the company, setting off a chain reaction causing other similar cases to be dismissed. He also brought a slander lawsuit against a man named Charles Luscombe, who apparently said that businessman Charles Herbert was "stealing shoes and selling them to niggers."

Now Mackey was ready to bring his most important case yet—cleaning up Alexandria County, which was in a desperate condition. Rosslyn and Jackson City were crowded with dangerous gambling houses. A racetrack near Del Ray was attracting a perilous crowd. Northern Virginia was becoming "the Monte Carlo of the East," a reputation that attracted violent criminals from Washington and Maryland. Dangerous characters roamed the streets. Farmers returning home from the market traveled in packs to avoid being robbed by highwaymen. Fear was in the air.

"Killings were commonplace, and cases were never brought to trial," wrote Arlington historian Eleanor Lee Templeman. "Saturday nights were particularly hazardous for the few law-abiding citizens who traversed the area en route home."

By the summer of 1903, Mackey was finally ready to take the plunge. Forged by years of involvement with progressive politics and muckraking legal cases, Mackey threw his hat into the ring to challenge incumbent Commonwealth's Attorney Richard Johnston, who was supported by the gambling interests. Before Mackey could take on Johnston, though, he had to win the support of progressives.

Three men were competing for a chance to challenge incumbent Johnston under the banner of the Good Citizens League, a loosely organized group of men interested in combating the influx of gambling establishments and infamous resorts. The youngest was a thirty-five-year-old lawyer from the Arlington District of Alexandria County, Frank Lyon. Then there was Will Douglas, a forty-two-year-old attorney who also lived in the Arlington magisterial district. Rounding out the candidates was Crandal Mackey, who was thirty-eight years old and the only candidate to live in the Washington District.

The nominating convention took place at the home of William Ball, a carpenter who was a leader of the nascent progressive movement in Alexandria County. Ball was patriarch to one of the most influential families in the region. His ancestors, John and Moses Ball, were among the earliest settlers of the area, acquiring property in the Glencarlyn area in the 1740s. Late in the eighteen century, a member of the family opened a tavern where the road to Alexandria crossed the road to Georgetown, which became known as Ball's Crossroads and, later, Ballston. There, on a crisp autumn evening in 1903, about twenty members of the Good Citizens League gathered in secret to nominate a commonwealth's attorney who would fight corruption.

"I remember the night well. It was a summer night," recalled Frank Ball, who was seventeen at the time. "Each one made a little speech and pledged to back the one selected by the group."

Then a crowd of "stern and determined men" gathered in the Ball parlor to deliberate. Lyon lived next door, so he went home. Douglas also went home. Mackey lingered in the oak grove behind the Ball home, chatting with the teenage Frank Ball. Mackey said that the young man should be a lawyer, adding that he might be able to help get a scholarship at the National University. "I don't know why he said that," said Ball. "But he did, and I had little idea along that line myself."

Meanwhile, inside the Ball parlor, deliberations were underway. "Their sole object was to select a candidate for commonwealth's attorney who would be a vote getter and would wreck the gamblers if elected," Ball recalled. "Of all the conventions or primaries this county has ever had, none was more important to our growth of well being."

Mackey was not the only candidate to challenge Johnston. Other challengers included Walter Varney and Richard Moncure, although Ball explained that they were just on the ballot to get their names known. A few weeks into the campaign, Moncure dropped out. His law partner was running for the Virginia

A 1903 campaign photo showing Crandal Mackey standing in front of Charlie Knoxville's Sunday bar. *Virginia Room, Arlington Public Library.*

Senate, and he figured that the law business would be irreparably harmed by two simultaneous campaigns. The real fight was between Johnston and Mackey, pitting the wealthy gambling interests against the progressive reformers.

"They had the doggonest knockdown dragout fight you ever saw in your life," recalled Ball in a 1964 speech to the Arlington Historical Society.

Mackey was supported by the anti-gambling element, a coalition that stayed together regardless of political affiliation. On the campaign trail, he pledged to drive the poolroom operators and the saloon sharks beyond the borders of Alexandria County. Traveling to the far reaches of the county in horse and buggy, Mackey made an effort to reach out to every voter who was not already in the pocket of the gambling interests. Mackey's home in the Washington District of Alexandria County, known as Rock Hill, was just one hundred yards west of Rosslyn, the hotbed of gambling and vice. If elected, Mackey promised, he would close every gambling resort in Alexandria.

"Mackey says Alexandria County has been the dumping grounds of all the riffraff and gamblers in Washington," the *Washington Times* reported.

"He proposes to make the place habitable so that the land can be sole and a higher standard of morals fixed."

Johnston, on the other hand, was supported by the forces of gambling. And money was flying in all directions. The *Washington Times* reported that barrels of money were opened, and their contents were "scattered in fabulous quantities." Everybody had money, although the dynamics of this election were different. Because of the Virginia's new constitution of 1902, blacks were subject to a new literacy test and a new poll tax. That meant a virtual elimination of the black vote, which was viewed by any progressive at the time as a corrupt faction of voters whose support could be purchased.

"The reduction of the negro vote, always a purchasable quantity, under the new Virginia constitution, helped Mackey wonderfully," the *Times* explained.

The gamblers were fighting for their lives, and there was no honor among thieves in these days. The syndicate that ran the big money operations in Northern Virginia had enemies all around, including many of the small-time gamblers they had cheated or run out of business. The unpopularity of the syndicate hurt Johnston, who ran one of the nastiest campaigns anyone could remember.

"The campaign was hotter than a firecracker," recalled Ball. "The gamblers fought with every political weapon they could muster, hitting below the belt more than above."

Every man, woman and child seemed to take an interest in the race, and the whole county was caught up. The *Washington Times* called the contest "one of the hottest local fights in the annals of Virginia politics." When all was said and done, the vote was very close. Johnston won the Arlington District and the Jefferson District by narrow margins. But Mackey's strong showing in the Washington District was enough to put him over the edge. Crandal Mackey ousted the incumbent with only *two votes*.

It was a mixed victory. William Palmer, who had been running for sheriff on the Johnston ticket, was elected despite the shift in the prosecutor's office. Almost immediately after the results were published in the newspapers, rumors began circulating that fifteen Alexandria County voters were planning to file a lawsuit against Mackey, challenging the results of the election. A week after election day, Walter Varney and Richard Johnston filed suit against Mackey, claiming "irregularities."

Essentially, the pair charged that Mackey controlled the election machinery in the county. Mackey denied the charges vigorously, and a court date was set with Judge James Love. Varney and Johnston wanted

The Alexandria County Courthouse was built in 1898. *Virginia Room, Arlington Public Library.*

Love to testify in the case, and they asked that another judge preside over the case. Love sent word to Governor Montague that another judge should be appointed. By the end of November, the governor had appointed Judge W.E. Lipscomb of Prince William County to oversee the case. And Love was indeed added to the witness list.

Each side began assembling a legal team in what was expected to be a knock-down, drag-out fight. Johnston was represented by a legal team that included some of the most powerful attorneys in Northern Virginia: Francis Smith, Edmund Burke and Charles Creighton Carlin. Mackey was represented by John Johnson, Walton Moore and Frank Lyon.

The Johnston legal team accused Mackey of buying eighteen votes, a violation of the "pure election law" of Virginia. The contest dragged on for three months of delays and procedural hearings. Newspapers reported that a number of men were prepared to testify that they were paid to vote for Mackey. But Mackey was able to provide evidence that the men were bearing false witness, proof that those willing to testify had actually voted for Johnston. By late December, Commonwealth's Attorney Johnston abruptly asked his attorneys to withdraw the contest.

"This, it is understood, will end the matter," reported the *Alexandria Gazette*.

Mackey took control of the prosecutor's office during a time of great tension between city and county. Alexandria became an independent city in 1870, separating itself from its more rural neighbors in the county. But even then, the county was already changing rapidly. From 1870 to 1900, census records show that the population of Alexandria tripled from 3,200 to 6,400. The two sister Alexandria governments had become uneasy neighbors. The county courthouse remained in the city until 1898, when a new courthouse was constructed in Alexandria County. The building faced Washington rather than Alexandria, perhaps an indication of how the county was changing at the time.

"Vice and crime were rampant and firmly entrenched here," Mackey recalled several years later. "The county was covered with gambling houses and Sunday bars. Every variety of crime including murder went unpunished. The black banners of official corruption floated over the county."

Ever since the end of the Civil War, chaos and disorder reigned in the county. By the turn of the century, lawless gang-established gambling houses, saloons and racetracks controlled Alexandria County. The trend was fueled in part by new methods of transportation, with a new trolley line opening in 1900. The line connected Clarendon, Ballston, Cherrydale, Bon Air, Glencarlyn and Barcroft.

Transportation was also at the center of one of the first fights between Mackey and the machine. In February 1904, a Southern Railway engineer named Cary Crump was in charge of an engine that ran into a carriage containing Bernard Brown and William Stokes. Mackey went after Crump, whose defense team was funded by powerful railroad interests. When the preliminary trial came before Justice Burrell at his house in the Jefferson District, none other than C.C. Carlin appeared for the defense. The trial was more than four hours long, and a large number of spectators showed up at the justice's house to hear the case. The justice declared Crump not guilty.

"As the accident occurred at a private crossing, and not a public one, the railway engineer had discharged his full duty as imposed upon him by law," Burrell concluded, according to the *Washington Times*. "Mr. Crump was tonight the recipient of many congratulations from his friends in this city on his acquittal."

In response to the increasing violence and disorder, a number of organizations were created. One of the most prominent was the Anti-Saloon League, created in 1893 by Congregationalist minister Howard Russell and Oberlin College student Wayne Wheeler. The organization was tightly focused on a single issue: banning the liquor traffic. The pragmatic movement would support "dry" candidates even if they were "wet" in their personal lives.

Wheeler invented the expression "pressure group," and he knew how to squeeze politicians into voting dry. In 1909, the organization moved to the Bliss Building on B Street (now known as Constitution Avenue) directly across the street from the United States Capitol. It was owned by Alonzo Bliss, a businessman who trafficked in medicinal marijuana and other herbal remedies. The building was later torn down and is now the location of the Robert Taft Memorial.

"There has never been an advocacy group quite like the Anti-Saloon League in American history, nor one as powerful," wrote historian Garrett Peck. "Not even the National Rifle Association is as powerful today as the ASL was in its heyday."

For Mackey and many of the other progressive leaders of the era, gambling and alcohol were vices joined at the hip. This was a time when the temperance movement was hardening into a prohibition movement—in part because of the wild excess that was plainly evident by scanning the crime column of the local papers.

"Prohibition as a political movement embodied various dimensions of progressivism," wrote Peter Wallenstein, "an organized attack on a social ill, a resort to legislation to address it, an effort to promote social welfare, and a reliance on social control."

The populists and the progressives struck an uneasy alliance with the prohibitionists. Together, they pushed for an income tax, popular election of senators, conservation of natural resources, trust-busting and regulation of the railroads. In city after city, municipal reformers were standing up to the machine. Tom Johnson cleaned out Cleveland. Mark Fagan took Jersey City. Sam "Golden Rule" Jones transformed Toledo. Now, Alexandria County had Crandal Mackey. This crop of local leaders saw the corrupting influence of power and money as ever-present dangers. But they had strong opposition. Ohio had Mark Hanna, and New York had Boss Thomas Platt. Journalist Lincoln Steffens outlined the struggle in his 1904 classic, "The Shame of the Cities."

"The spirit of graft and lawlessness is the American spirit," Steffens wrote. "We break our own laws and rob our own government, the lady at the customhouse, the lyncher with his rope, and the captain of industry with his bride and his rebate."

At its heart, the progressive movement that Crandal Mackey joined was a reaction to the mounting urban evils, which were violently apparent at the bottom of Dead Man's Hollow. Part of it was an old-school sense of humanitarianism the likes of which led churches of the era to sponsor settlement houses. Another part of it was very modern, reflecting the growing new science of sociology. Together, the dueling faces of the movement created a powerful force for political change.

As early as 1895, the Anti-Saloon League was charging publically that the liquor business maintained an unholy alliance with organized crime and machine politics. Now, as Crandal Mackey assumed the reins of power at the Alexandria County Courthouse, he had a mandate to fight against the social evils of public drunkenness, gambling politicians and rapacious corporations.

For many years, the standard view of this era was that it was a time when the people subdued the special interests, statesmen overwhelmed the political bosses and altruistic reformers cleaned out government corruption. That view has been challenged in recent decades as more have come to see the era as a series of conflicts between special-interest groups. The current thinking on the Progressive era is that it was a time when professionalization and bureaucratization triggered the reform impulse, not quixotic altruism.

Crandal Mackey is a reflection of the change that was happening at the dawn of the twentieth century. Reformers of the era were being shaped by events even as they set out to change the world. As people like Mackey took office, an important transformation was taking place. The ragtag amateurs were becoming skilled operators who knew the tricks of the trade, although they faced serious opposition from an entrenched machine. Almost immediately after his election, Mackey started calling for a crackdown on crime and corruption. But it wouldn't be that easy.

"He called on law enforcement officers to demand a clean-out of the gambling dens, but the sheriff asked for more time," explained Arlington historian Eleanor Lee Templeman. "When no action had been taken in four months, Captain Mackey addressed letters to thirty citizens asking them to meet at four o'clock on May 30 at his law office in Washington to form a posse to accompany him in raiding the dens."

The fight was on. Armed with a posse of supporters and a shotgun, Mackey decided to strike out on his own. Alexandria County would never be the same.

FORGOTTEN JACKSON CITY

Don't look for it today. It's gone. Most people have never heard of it and probably wouldn't believe you if you told them. Jackson City was a place for policy writing, crap shooting, faro dealing and running the sweatboard. It was also a hotbed of prostitution and murder.

"It was the very bottom of hell," recalled Frank Ball. "You couldn't get any lower."

One infamous spot at Jackson City earned the nickname Hell's Bottom.

"It was the execution spot for those who did not cooperate with the gang leaders," wrote Arlington historian Eleanor Lee Templeman. "Hangings took place on an average of one every week."

Nothing remains of Jackson City except the cornerstone laid by President Andrew Jackson. And even that has been obscured by the Navy-Marine Memorial. These days, Jackson City has been totally forgotten. But when Crandal Mackey was elected commonwealth's attorney in 1903, cleaning up Jackson City was at the top of the agenda.

"Nobody can tell you about Jackson City and degrade it any," said Ball. "It was so degraded it couldn't get any lower."

Calling it a city at all was somewhat of a joke. There were no streets, roads or sidewalks. Nobody ever heard of a marriage license. It started as a dream and ended up a nightmare. The area had once been known as Nameroughquena by the Necostin Indians. Captain John Smith put it on the map after his visit in 1608, although the area eventually became known as Holmes Island. It later became part of the Alexander estate and

The Navy Marine Memorial was constructed over the old cornerstone of Jackson City. *Brandy Crist-Travers.*

became known as Alexander's Island. In 1835, a group of wealthy New York speculators had their eyes on a stretch of waterfront in Alexandria, D.C. Hoping to capitalize on the construction of the Long Bridge, as well as the Washington-Alexandria Turnpike and Columbia Turnpike, they created a joint stock company. Daniel Jackson, William Rockwell and Henry Wilkes put their signatures on the document in the presence of New York City Mayor Cornelius Lawrence, an indication that the project had a sense of great expectations.

But those expectations never met reality. The tract of land was a 550-acre plot acquired by Richard Mason that had formerly been owned by Philip Alexander, part of the family that the city was named after. The deed book describes the land as "all that Island in the River Potomac opposite the City of Washington and originally known by the name of Holmes Island but of late more commonly distinguished by the name Alexander's Island, being connected with said city by the bridge and causeway lately constructed over the said river by the government of the United States and with the mainland on the opposite side by the causeway of the Washington and Alexandria Turnpike Co, and the mainland contiguous thereto."

The speculators hoped to "lay off and develop the same into squares, lots, streets and ways for selling, renting, or otherwise disposing of the same." Once that was accomplished, the businessmen would "build and erect warehouses, stores, dwellings and wharves on the same and make other improvements." A harbor was dredged out, and hope soared that the new port would rival Alexandria and Georgetown as a shipping point.

The river basin would "admit vessels of the largest class engaged in foreign trade." Situated at the mouth of Gravelly Creek, the harbor separated the island from the mainland. The speculators hired an engineer who was obviously impressed.

"There can scarcely be a more beautiful position for a city than these grounds afford," he concluded.

The name of this place was to be Jackson City, thought to be a nod to President Andrew Jackson, who had survived an assassination attempt at the Capitol earlier that year by beating the tar of his assailant. It's possible that the name might have been a reference to one of the investors. Then again, it's possible that it may have been named for both. Or neither.

In any event, the foundation stone was laid on January 11, 1836. The event featured a great deal of the kind of pomp and circumstance popular in the era. President Jackson was attended. George Washington Parke Custis, who was at the time living in the Arlington House haunting the top of the hill, addressed the crowd. One contemporaneous account described it as a "bright, bracing January morning" filled with "drums beating, cannon firing, plates clattering and corks drawing." The event "made the high and low turn out and filled the mud banks…with a greater crowd than it ever bore before or ever will again."

The foundation stone that was laid that day, the one that's now hidden under the Navy-Marine Memorial, consisted of two seats of perishable freestone. One was sunk in the earth with a hole cut for reception of a box, and the other was slung by pulleys above. The box was deposited and the slab was lowered. President Jackson gave it three knocks with a small gilt hammer. Then the Masons gave nine claps with their hands. Artillery thundered in the crisp January air. "Humbug City, unlike Rome, was built in a day," observed Arlington historian Eleanor Lee Templeman.

Across the Potomac River, abolitionists presented a petition to Congress. South Carolina Senator John C. Calhoun responded that the petition was a "foul slander" of the South. The famously ill-tempered Jackson may have reacted more violently if he were there in person, so perhaps it was fortuitous that he was in Alexandria, D.C., at the ceremony creating Jackson

City. As the drums beat that day, nobody could have known the fate of this venture. In fact, it's a safe bet that nobody would have ever guessed what would become of Jackson City.

"This city was to become an industrial twin city to Washington, with a seaport in the excavated basin in the swamp, which is now Roach's Run Bird Sanctuary," wrote Templeman.

But that's not what happened. Almost immediately, the land was on the auction block. A trustee of the late Richard Mason offered the entire five-hundred-acre property at a public auction, when the tract was described as fertile farm and garden land, suitable for dairy farming and as a cattle stand. In order to be successful, though, the city needed a charter from Congress. This stretch of waterfront, after all, was part of the District of Columbia at the time. But the established interests in Alexandria and Georgetown stood in strong opposition to such a charter. And even without Congressional representation for either city, the effort of the investors to secure a charter went down in flames.

"The Alexandria and Georgetown men were not enthusiastic, as its success would take business from their own wharves and warehouses," wrote Templeman. "Hence, their newspapers threw sarcastic and caustic editorial jibes at what they termed the speculative hoax of Humbug City."

The dream of creating a respectable community had already come to an end by the turn of the century. No charter was ever issued, and no roads were ever built. It remained farmland for many years until a ramshackle racetrack was constructed on a part of the property that would later become Ronald Reagan Washington National Airport.

It was a settlement of derelict structures that looked as though they could fall over in a strong wind. For years, the only improvement to the tract was a "comfortable dwelling house" and a cattle stand, where the animals watered on the way to District markets. Although Jackson City had its own stop on the railroad, the platform was uncovered and had none of the ornamentation that other stations of the era boasted. It was called, simply, "South end of Long Bridge."

"Jackson City is such in name only. It has not even an official existence," reported the *Washington Post*. "It has no post office, and the name of this place is itself a joke."

The Civil War changed the fate of Jackson City, which was transformed from a pastoral farmland to a gambler's paradise. First, New Jersey promoters moved in after gambling was outlawed in their state. Then, Washington, D.C., outlawed gambling, and Jackson City really took off. Some of the

Jackson City was located on the Virginia side of the Long Bridge. *Virginia Room, Arlington Public Library.*

bookmakers moved to Seventh Street beyond the District boundary, but many others moved into the commonwealth.

"The bookmakers who have moved over to Jackson City say they have no fear of being disturbed by the Virginia authorities," the *Post* reported shortly after Congress passed a law banning gambling in D.C. "Doubtless before the week is ended every one of the bookmakers heretofore out at the boundary will have either found or built quarters over the bridge in Virginia."

By the 1890s, a wire had been installed to three other pool betting rooms, and operators sat at the telegraph waiting to take down entries. The settlement had about half a dozen wooden buildings, a watch box for the railroad employee who was unfortunate enough to be stationed there and bitter memories.

"Out of nine buildings that constitute this unique settlement, there is only one that is used for legitimate purposes," explained the *Washington Star*. "The other eight are given over to those who follow fickle fortune on the green baize cloth."

A visit to Jackson City was not likely to carry any fond remembrances, especially since many unlucky poor men and young clerks on small salaries were forced to walk home because they no longer had money for a streetcar ticket. The ghosts of Jackson City were penniless and pitiless, lost souls stripped of their dignity and their pocket change. Hell's Bottom may have been a generous description for the destitution created here.

"Many a gay blade from Washington lost his fortune there to walk home over Long Bridge with empty pockets," wrote Templeman. "Lawless elements ruled local politics."

A wagon road ran down the left side of the tracks, and a raggedy line of two-story buildings was on the right. From the outside, the frame buildings looked like any roadhouse or saloon. But step inside, and visitors found an exciting thrill.

"They had the most beautiful furniture you ever saw and wonderful paintings," recalled Frank Ball. "Not the kind you would want to hang on your parlor walls, but paintings just the same."

Here, visitors could enter a different world, one that was separated from the everyday concerns and one that offered the promise of wealth and prestige. "Step right up, gentlemen, and place your bets," the dealer would belt. "The horses are at the post and all bets will close in a minute."

Unlike in the District of Columbia, where lynx-eyed watchmen guarded the door to make sure that applicants for admission were members of a charmed circle, anyone and everyone was welcomed at Jackson City. Nothing more substantial than a swinging saloon door guarded the entrance. One man's money was as good as another.

"There are no distinctions made on account of class or color," the *Washington Star* explained. "The dapper government clerk or the clubman out of an experience stands a very good chance of brushing up against the boy who blacked his boots earlier in the day."

The *Star* sent a reporter and an artist to capture the scene at Jackson City in 1892. What they discovered was the best available version of the truth, a sort of travelogue of drinking and gambling that paints a vivid picture of what life was like at Jackson City in its heyday.

"It is a happy-go-lucky sort of a crowd, and there is little of that tense subdued excitement that one is familiar with in storybook descriptions of gambling houses," the *Star* reported. "There is no visible feverish greed for gain, though occasionally when the wrong horse is telegraphed as the winner, one hears remarks about 'going dead broke again,' or words to that effect."

The newspaper set the scene for what it was like at Jackson City, a place where visitors could play the races, faro, craps, raffle, sweatboard and even a dice game known as "chuck-a-luck." Along one side of the room was a large blackboard, where entries and odds were written in chalk. In the back of the room was a bar, where beer and whiskey were served. On the other side of the room was the telegraph machine, chugging and whirring along with information about horse races in Guttenburg and Gloucester.

"The crowd in the pool rooms know just as well what is going on in Guttenburg and Gloucester as if they were there in person," the *Star* reported. "They know the condition of the weather and of the track, and they are able to follow the race in detail from the time the horses are called to the post until the winner and the time are announced."

The fact-finding mission began with a cab ride. The mere mention of the destination is all the cabman needed. Apparently, he did not need to be told directions because he had driven many other pairs of young men to the same place about the same time of day, when federal offices shut down for the afternoon. When they arrived, the *Star* correspondents heard a good deal of talk about probable winners. When someone had a sure thing, his standing skyrocketed. And when someone was unlucky, they fell from grace just as fast.

"No sooner is one race run than the betting on the next one begins, and there is something to do all the time," the *Star* explained. "The interest is not allowed to flag for a moment."

For those who were more ambitious, above one of the poolrooms was a large apartment where faro and roulette were played. Here, the smallest chips retailed for a quarter, and the game was considerably more respectable. Faro was a game that was very popular with the late-night crowd, as well as with those who arrived from the city to while away the hours and a few dollars.

"The room is comfortably furnished and lighted," the *Star* reported. "A large sideboard at one end of it is stocked with liquors that are at the service of patrons of the house."

When the newspaper reporter and artist arrived in the high-roller suite above the poolroom that January afternoon, apparently things were relatively quiet. The evening's fun had not yet begun, and all they found was two mechanics playing faro. They were not green at the game, the newspaper reported, and what they knew about it could not be learned for a dollar. Suddenly, a young man about twenty years old entered the room and began to gamble. He was well dressed and just starting out in the world. He bought five dollars worth of chips.

"By conscientious playing and strict attention to the game, he managed to lose it all in about ten minutes," the newspaper reported. "Then he got up and started to leave, for it was all the money he had."

But that wasn't the end of the story.

"Won't you have a drink before you go," asked the dealer.

Hell's Bottom. *Virginia Room, Arlington Public Library.*

"Thank you. I think I'll not take any," he responded. "I don't know, though. I believe I will take a little whiskey."

With that, the attendant took a large bottle and a small glass out of the sideboard. The young man poured out a drink "that would have answered every purpose for an old drinker." The young man drank it down until water came into his eyes, "for it was more than he had ever drank before." Then he started on his long, cold walk home—cursing Jackson City and vowing never to return again. But he would. Again and again.

"The dream may have faded," observed Arlington historian Cornelia Rose. "But this area of Arlington County was known as Jackson City well into the 20th century."

Jackson City may have been Hell's Bottom or Humbug City, but it was very popular. The *Washington Post* reported that Jackson City logged about two thousand daily visitors from Washington and Baltimore. They came to buy pools and indulge in other forms of gambling.

"They didn't have anything there except speakeasies and gambling places, one or two licensed saloons and a lot of lewd women—everything rough,"

Frank Ball recalled. "Nobody lived there except the keepers of those places who lived in the upstairs rooms."

Newspapers from the era are full of harrowing dispatches from Jackson City. "Passengers, ladies and gentlemen who traveled on the trains passing Jackson City were insulted by Washington gamblers," the *Washington Post* reported in 1892. "There were instances where drunken gamesters had hugged ladies on some of these trains."

This was the mess that Crandal Mackey was elected to clean up, transforming the "Monte Carlo of Virginia" from Hell's Bottom into something more respectable.

"Gradually, Commonwealth's Attorney Mackey, of Alexandria county, is weaving his net around the gang of gamblers whose presence at the south end of Long Bridge had long caused Alexandria county to be considered one of the toughest spots in Virginia," the *Washington Times* reported. "If he keeps up his present vigorous warfare, the time is not far distant when Jackson City and Rosslyn will both be models of virtue."

THE HIDDEN HISTORY OF ROSSLYN

Vice. Saloons. Gambling houses. Brothels. It's hard to believe it today, but Rosslyn once had it all.

That's all gone now. No trace of it is left today. These days, the neighborhood is known for looming skyscrapers and cavernous Metro corridors. If people know anything about Rosslyn, it's that *Washington Post* reporter Bob Woodward met his undercover source from the Federal Bureau of Investigation known as "Deep Throat" in an underground garage here. Today, visitors find the glamorous Key Bridge but no trace of the spooky old Aqueduct Bridge that it replaced. Modern-day Rosslyn bears no trace of its shady past, a time when crime and murder was so common here that Rosslyn was home to a spot known as Dead Man's Hollow.

"Some committed suicide. Some were killed by gamblers and the liquor people," recalled Frank Ball. "Some got in fights and a little bit of everything happened."

Filed away in the dusty backroom shelves of the Virginia Room at Arlington Central Library is a collection of faded photographs that tells the story of Rosslyn. Rich in sepia tones and jagged edges, the images seem haunted by ghosts of a Rosslyn that many people wanted to forget. The series offers a kind of tour of a forgotten place.

There's the old Klondike place, which ran wide open in Rosslyn on Sunday in open violation of blue laws. To the rear of the building, justices of the peace and minor officers of the county arrived every Monday to pick up envelopes full of cash. Over on Columbia Pike and Mount Vernon Avenue

County officials picked up envelopes full of cash at the old Klondike place. *Virginia Room, Arlington Public Library.*

was a notorious resort operated by Mitt Johnson, who was chairman of the County Excise Board. He granted licenses to himself and other lawbreakers. Then there was Tillie Dennison Place and the Woltz Place and the Sunday bar that operated out of the back of an African American church.

It wasn't always like this. The hidden history of Rosslyn begins in 1860, when Joseph Lambden purchased the property and deeded a substantial portion of it to his daughter Carolyn and her husband William Henry Ross. They called it Rosslyn.

Opinions are divided as to how the name came about. One story suggests that it's a combination of the name Ross and the word "lyn," an obsolete spelling of "linn" (a word describing the torrent of water rushing over the rocks in the Potomac River). Another story is that the name Rosslyn combines the name Ross and "lyn" from the name Carolyn.

However it got the name, Rosslyn would eventually become synonymous with tramps, embezzlers, thieves, housebreaks, murders and criminals of all kind. As Arlington historian Eleanor Lee Templeman put it, Rosslyn was "a gateway to perdition."

"No western mining town was ever wilder, until the gambling interests were driven out," added Templeman.

A group of barrooms in Rosslyn. *Virginia Room, Arlington Public Library.*

The area was first explored by Captain John Smith, the famed English explorer who searched the Chesapeake Bay for a passage to the Pacific Ocean in 1608. Instead, he found a band of American Indians, probably belonging to the Necostin tribe. The earliest land records of Rosslyn date to 1657, granting "the freshes of the Pawtomack above Anacosta Iland." The land was swapped by English nobility, including Lord Culpepper and Lord Fairfax. European settlement here began in the mid-1700s, centering on three ferries that crossed the Potomac River and provided access to colonists from Maryland. One of those ferries landed on the seventy-five-acre Awbrey plantation, which is about a mile below modern-day Key Bridge.

By the 1760s, almost all of what we now think of as Northern Virginia was Fairfax County. And much of what we think of as the United States was Northern Virginia. Maps from this era show three main roads radiating out of the area we now call Rosslyn. Ferries provided the only way of crossing the river until 1797, when a bridge was constructed on the site of the modern-day Chain Bridge. The District of Columbia was in the process of being created at the time, although Georgetown and Alexandria were already thriving port cities.

Cunningham's Sunday bar in Rosslyn. *Virginia Room, Arlington Public Library.*

By the time Rosslyn became part of the original District of Columbia, it was still a rural backwater. Very few residents were around to complain about a takeover, and so the takeover happened with very little complaining—at least in Rosslyn. The folks in Old Town Alexandria did quite a bit of complaining, and they got the Virginia side of the district retroceded back to the Old Dominion in 1847.

When the Civil War erupted, the Ross family skipped town. What had once been a bucolic setting was transformed into a war zone, complete with three Union forts. Most of the civilian population left in an effort to flee the horrors of war, the unpleasantness of conscripted soldiers and the hassle of acquiring a military pass just to travel to the market.

An 1865 map showing the defenses of Washington bears the name "Rosslyn" for the first time, along with a series of buildings that were part of the federal occupation. When it became clear that the occupation would be indefinite, the Ross family moved to France and sold the farm to the Rosslyn Development Company.

And yet even after the war, Rosslyn retained a wartime atmosphere. Fort Whipple remained fully occupied, with Union soldiers guarding the post even as Virginia was struggling its way through Reconstruction. It was named after Brevet Major General Amiel Weeks Whipple, who was killed at the Battle of Chancellorsville. By 1881, it had been renamed Fort Myer after Brigadier General Albert Myer, who established the Signal School of Instruction.

The soldiers who were stationed here had a love-hate relationship with their neighbors in Rosslyn. It's pretty clear that many of them visited the Old Bachelor Roadhouse, conveniently located at the entrance of the fort. It was the best little whorehouse in Rosslyn, an "all-night house" where "dissolute women" collected. When the soldiers were in a fighting mood, they would head over to Gary's Sunday bar and gambling place. This was the scene of a riot in 1903, when one of the soldiers was shot in the back. Hundreds of soldiers showed up and shut the place down.

It was a place of desperation where thirty-year-old Adele Shilling attempted suicide in 1903. The clerk of the secondhand store on D Street Northwest was struck by the woman's "peculiar demeanor" when she bought a revolver. He managed to send word to detectives, who learned that she was suffering from an incurable disease and that she did not care to live. No wonder she was attracted to Rosslyn; she was found aimlessly wandering the streets there with a revolver.

What had been farmlands and pastures before the war was transformed into the Wild West. As for the town, there wasn't much of one beyond the saloons, bordellos, gambling institutions and houses of ill repute. For many years, commerce in Rosslyn was limited to a lumberyard, a winery, a lithograph print shop and a brick factory. Criminals lurked in the shadows, and nobody knew when the next body would be dumped in Dead Man's Hollow.

"No man ventured away from his home unarmed," wrote Arlington historian George Gills.

The only landmark to speak of was the Consumer Brewing Company, founded in 1890 on the banks of the Potomac River where the Rosslyn Marriott now stands. By 1897, the company had constructed a massive new building here. It was designed by prominent local architect Albert Goenner, who also built the Alexandria Country Courthouse in 1898. The brewery was a large red brick building, with turrets at each end, a clock tower in the center and a large smokestack. It made light lager, a dark lager, ale and a porter, much of which was consumed in the saloons of Rosslyn.

The imposing structure must have made quite an impression from the banks of Georgetown, where people in the District could peer across the Potomac and see this Gothic monument to beer. It was constructed using

George Woltz's bar. *Virginia Room, Arlington Public Library.*

the industrial brickyards along the Potomac River, and bricklayers placed several horseshoes and a mule shoe at the top of the brewery smokestack for luck. It advertised that it would deliver its products within the local area for free, and deliveries were made with an unmarked wagon.

Advertising beer on a wagon would have been asking for trouble on the dangerous streets of Rosslyn, where highwaymen lurked in the dark. Farmers traveling to the market were terrified of being confronted, so they would travel in armed convoys. Murders would happen every week, if not more frequently.

"I've seen farmers come through Rosslyn Saturday nights coming back from Washington market afraid to come through by themselves," recalled Frank Ball. "Five or six would get in a line and everyone of them had a sawed-off shotgun in his wagon coming home from the market."

The situation in Rosslyn was appalling to many reform-minded people, who began organizing temperance reforms aimed at the village. The press called the efforts "dry Sunday," an effort to enforce Virginia's blue laws. The first such temperance campaign happened in 1900. Another was organized in 1902, when Sheriff William Palmer marched into town early one Sunday morning in August with his armed posse of twelve deputies.

Tillie Dennison's Sunday bar. *Virginia Room, Arlington Public Library.*

"The sheriff's posse had a lonely time of it in the town, with nothing to do but fight away vast swarms of mosquitoes," the *Washington Times* reported. "But they kept the saloons closed up tight, and inaugurated a red-letter day in the village across the river."

Not a drop of liquor was sold. Not a single fight broke out. People in search of a drink headed up the hill in droves, out of Rosslyn. "Never in the memory of even the oldest inhabitants has such a complete quiet existed," the *Times* noted. "The few loafers who remained in town strolled aimlessly about like the proverbial Rip Van Winkle, unable to recognize their native town."

The village storekeeper sat on his porch, stroking his mustache and surveying the scene. The village parson made the rounds, but the unruly hamlet had become a ghost town. Blacks gathered at a stand to eat ice cream and pigs' feet. Rosslyn was as quiet as a city of the dead as the sheriff's deputies sat on the stoop of each saloon. "We are keeping Rosslyn dry," an unnamed deputy told the *Times*. "Unless there is a speakeasy being operated in some of the houses, there is absolutely no liquor to be had in Rosslyn today."

When an artilleryman stationed at Fort Myer Heights was shot while passing through Rosslyn in 1902, soldiers descended on James Geary's saloon and started a riot. The place was wrecked, and damages were estimated at $2,000. Twelve soldiers were arrested, and a court of inquiry was convened at Fort Myer. The *Washington Times* reported that Geary may have been targeted because he was not willing to contribute bribes to the political ring that ran the political scene.

The situation remained tense. By the summer of 1903, Alexandria County Judge James Love had ruled that the state courts have no jurisdiction to make arrests on the reservation because it was government land entirely under the control of the United States government. That decision prompted the War Department to send two squads of soldiers, infantrymen and cavalry from Fort Myer to camp on five acres of government land at the south end of the Aqueduct Bridge. They were there to preserve a tenuous peace and prevent rioting, but their presence made the situation even more anxious.

This appalled Frank Lyon, a young and ambitious lawyer and friend of Crandal Mackey. In 1903, he was one of the three candidates vying to become the progressive candidate to unseat the corrupt incumbent, Richard Johnston. Lyon came to Virginia in 1889, settling west of Kirkwood Road near the William Ball house. When Lyon's children walked to school in the morning, they took their own lives in their hands when they walked through Rosslyn on their way to Georgetown. If they didn't make the right connections on the way home, they would have to wait up to an hour for the next train from Rosslyn.

Lyon decided that he didn't want to just complain about the situation; he wanted to do something about it. So, he purchased a newspaper called the *Rosslyn Monitor*. Although much of the *Monitor* has been lost to history, some issues survive. Its pages help tell the story of how Crandal Mackey cleaned up Rosslyn, one whorehouse and saloon at a time.

"Frank Lyon pioneered in the establishment of this county as a residential community," wrote Arlington historian Eleanor Lee Templeman. "Both Lyon Park and Lyon Village, which he later developed, perpetuate his name. Throughout Northern Virginia, his series of handsome residences, including Lyonhurst at 4651 25th Street North are monuments to his versatile architectural taste."

Working together with Lyon and other members of the Good Citizens League, Crandal Mackey transform Rosslyn—a personal crusade of sorts considering that Mackey called the neighborhood home. The Rosslyn that Mackey inherited that January day in 1904 was a dirty and dangerous place, where people from the District would arrive on one of sixteen Washington and Old Dominion Railway trains each day.

GENTLEMAN'S DRIVING CLUB

The St. Asaph Racetrack offered more than a cheap bottle of booze or an easy lady of the night. It had glamour and money. Wealth and power. Graft and greed. Political corruption and telegraph wires. St. Asaph was no saint.

Asaph is a Hebrew word for "God has gathered," but it might as well have meant "pay your bets" in Alexandria County, where the St. Asaph Racetrack was the capital of gambling in Northern Virginia. It connected two railroad neighborhoods, Del Ray to the south and St. Elmo to the north. The track originally opened in 1894, although Virginia outlawed horse racing in 1897.

That didn't matter much at St. Asaph, where rules were meant to be broken. Betting on the races at the track was never as profitable as betting on the races elsewhere, thanks to the track's infamous poolroom, where gamblers could receive a steady stream of information from the telegraph wires. In its heyday, the operation was making as much as $150,000 per year—even after paying $14,000 a year for telegraph service and $12,000 a year in graft to local officials.

It all started so innocently. Horse racing dates back to the earliest days of the city. As early as 1760, the *Maryland Gazette* carried an announcement that a horse race would be run "at the usual race-ground near Alexandria." The purse was thirty pounds, the best of three heats. In 1786, the *Alexandria Gazette* reported that horses named Paul Jones and Slippery Jack were recent winners "at the Alexandria course." One of the city's earliest social organizations was the Jockey Club, which met regularly at Gadsby's Tavern for rum and camaraderie.

The St. Asaph Racetrack. *Virginia Room, Arlington Public Library.*

A 1799 advertisement in the *Alexandria Times* indicated that the track was in the northern part of the town near the turnpike, what is now known as Jefferson Davis Highway. That area was later used again as a racetrack in the mid-nineteenth century, when horses named Boston, Wilton Brown and Prior competed for the best two of three.

After the Civil War, gambling saloons exploded across Washington, D.C. Senators and congressman could be seen freely coming and going from gambling houses, a phenomenon that must have caused some sense of embarrassment. After a few high-profile problems with customers who were unwilling or unable to pay their debts, Congress took action and outlawed gambling in the District of Columbia.

That moved attention across the Potomac River into Alexandria. Rosslyn and Jackson City became the immediate benefactors because of their choice locations at the Virginia end of the two major bridges. But the big money was focused at Potomac Yard, the massive industrial train yard that dominated the landscape north of Alexandria.

Two neighborhoods had already sprouted up near the train yards. Del Ray was laid out in a grid pattern in 1894. To the north, St. Elmo offered a similar grid on a smaller scale. The two neighborhoods were oriented along east–west roads that connected Mount Vernon Avenue on the west, with the Washington-Alexandria Turnpike on the east. The longer blocks running east to west allowed the house gardens to get a maximum amount of sun. But danger lurked in the shadows.

The St. Asaph Racetrack became the center of an ongoing feud between the Jones family and the Hill family. It was a feud that dated back to 1885, when Orlando Jones opened a poolroom in the Imperial Hotel in Washington, D.C. The operation flourished, in part because the District of Columbia had no laws against poolrooms in those days. Senators and congressmen were frequent guests, although the gambling industry brought its own sense of morality.

Violence and double-crossing were the order of the day. Members of Congress became concerned and outlawed gambling in the District, which had the effect of sending a massive influx of people to the two bridges leading to Virginia—the Aqueduct Bridge leading to Rosslyn and the Long Bridge leading to Jackson City. When the time came to settle with the house, not everyone was willing or able to pay the check. One establishment, known as the Marble Saloon, was run by the infamous Frank Ward, who once killed a man rather than let him leave without paying off his debt. When another Washington gambling house under the name of Bliss & Company failed for $3,000, rival Harry Howard posted a notice on the blackboard of the Marble poolroom announcing that all outstanding tickets would be cashed at his establishment.

The idea that eventually became the St. Asaph Racetrack had its origins back in 1888, when the Gentleman's Driving Club was chartered. By 1893, leaders in Virginia had become alarmed about gambling in the commonwealth. So, the General Assembly began talking about following suit. Here is where greed and graft enter the picture, corrupting the process and greasing the levers of power. Alexandria County gamblers traveled to Richmond to buttonhole legislators in a bid to carve out an exemption that could give them a competitive advantage. It worked. Corrupt legislators ended up adding a provision creating an exemption for driving clubs, agricultural organizations or grange associations.

That's when the Jones brothers began investing in a racetrack at Jackson City. Now that the General Assembly had created a loophole wide enough to guide a racehorse through, the brothers procured the charter of the Grange Camp Association of Virginia.

But the Jones family wasn't alone. The Hill family was also interested in cashing in on the new law. They bought the charter for the Alexandria

Driving Park at St. Asaph. Like two warring families in a Shakespearean drama, the rival clans did everything in their power to undercut each other. The Jones faction tried to prevent the Hill brothers from building the St. Asaph track, and the Hill family tried to retaliate by having the Jones brothers arrested.

The Hills were more than able to keep up with the Jonses, especially considering the list of influential people who were in on the deal. Trustees of the Alexandria Driving Park included some of the most prominent men in town: William Daingerfield, Reverdy Daingerfield, George Uhler, Park Agnew and Virginia Senator George Mushback. John Marriott Hill, who managed the city's opera house and a printing establishment, was in charge of the betting. Livery stable owner James Patterson became the chief promoter. Investors dumped $100,000 into making the facility a first-class endeavor.

By the spring of 1894, the park was almost ready to open. For months, a large force of men had been working feverishly to prepare for opening day. Stables were constructed for the horses, and offices were built for the proprietors. Broad porticoes were attached to an old farmhouse, which was transformed into a dining room and restaurant. Originally known as the Gentlemen's Driving Park at St. Asaph Junction, the facility featured an oval-shaped track with large grounds. It was obviously a smashing success.

"Bookies are doing a rushing business," reported the *Washington Post*. "The old poolroom at the track is crowded every day with Washington sports anxious to place their money on horses running on the St. Louis or New Orleans tracks."

Within the first month of opening day in March 1894, the owners were already talking about expanding. By October, promoters were ready to start the fall season. The track began referring to itself as St. Asaph because it was near the St. Asaph junction, which can be seen on a colorful insurance map from 1900. In October, the racetrack thumped to life with forty days of continuous racing. That season was significant because the owners wanted to be clear that they were in no way sanctioning winter racing. The promoters envisioned the two and a half months as an extension of the regular season in the North, transferring it to a sunnier and warmer climate during the autumn.

It had its own electric plant to generate lighting, twelve thousand feet of pipe to get running water from Alexandria, a stable that could accommodate three hundred horses and a grandstand that could seat 3,000 spectators. On an average day, the track would attract about 1,800 people. A field of clover was planted in the infield. Horses had names such as White Cockade,

Westmoreland, Happy Jim, Happy Sally, Devenish, and Florence D. The official starter was James Rowe, despite the best efforts of Snapper Garrison, who wanted the honor of holding the flag at the new track.

Although promoters billed the facility as a three-quarter track, it was a mile from the head of the chute around the course, which was ninety feet wide in the shape of a figure six. Journalists from all over the region traveled to the Jockey Club and gushed about its beauty. It was an operation owned by the leading businessmen of the era, with stables representing the fairest sport imaginable. Former Mayor Emanuel Downham was the president of the club.

"So far as location is concerned the track…is situated in a sort of punch bowl formation," the *Washington Post* exclaimed, "the heaven-kissing hills of Maryland and Virginia forming the sides."

Its inaugural season had six races every day for forty days, with the first race starting at 1:45 p.m. Racing enthusiasts marveled at the excellent turf, scratching their heads at how the facility could have perfected it in such a short amount of time. Owners dropped more than $100,000 to create the turf, fit the grandstand and build the stables. Purses ranged from $400 to $700. Each jockey had a $250 entrance fee, with the winner taking $4,000 and the second $1,000.

Six races took place each afternoon, beginning at 2:00 p.m. No more than fifteen horses were racing at a time. Each race was required to have three horses not trained by the same man. An *Alexandria Gazette* article from 1894 described the racetrack as "one of the prettiest driving parks in the country."

"The track is certainly a fine one, the buildings are handsome and commodious and many more are to be erected—all with an eye to architectural beauty," the *Gazette* added. "It is the purpose of the managers to make the place one of the most attractive driving parks in the country and the fastest horses are to be run there."

Much of the racetrack's success was due to its location. The three-quarters-of-a-mile track was situated on the railroad between the North and the South. Special trains left the Washington and Baltimore station in Washington every weekday when the races were taking place. In November 1895, the railroad advertised sixteen daily round trips, from 6:30 a.m. to 9:30 p.m.

Ferries also departed from the foot of Seventh Street in Washington and landed in Alexandria, where passengers would be transported by the Mount Vernon Electric Railway directly to the grandstand of the racetrack.

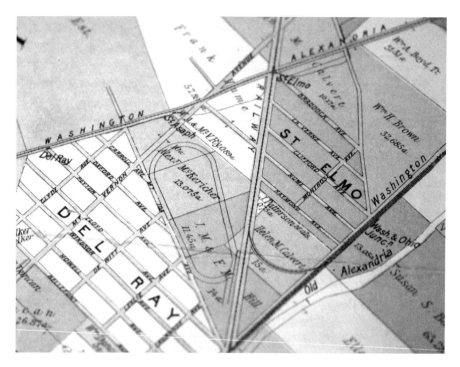

A 1900 insurance map showing the location of the racetrack, separating the Del Ray neighborhood from St. Elmo. *Alexandria Library Local History Special Collections*

Commuters from Washington could get there in twenty minutes, and residents of Alexandria could get there before they knew how much money they were going to bet. An advertisement in the *Washington Post* explained that the train to Washington would leave "immediately after the last race."

"It is as pretty a picture as one could imagine to sit in the spacious, comfortable and well-arranged grand stand and take in the surrounding country," the *Washington Post* noted. "During the interregnum between the races the spectators' eyes will find relief in the verdure clad hills, which stretch far away to the limit of the range of vision until they form an irregular outline silhouetted against the horizon."

For visitors, the park offered a panorama of sorts. On the right, visitors could see the hills of Virginia. On the left, in the distance, the Maryland shore was visible. And there, smack dab in the center, was the Potomac River. Because of the arrangement of the stables and grandstand, which faced south, the horses were never out of sight. Horses and guests alike had access to the best and purest water around. President Emanuel Downham and Secretary H.D. McIntyre made it clear that this organization was going to be legitimate by hiring "a strong force" of Pinkerton detectives to work the betting lawn and grandstand.

"No improper character will be permitted within the enclosure," the *Washington Post* reported, "the dominant idea of the promoters of this enterprise being that the ladies and gentlemen can attend the races without the slightest fear of being brought in contact with obnoxious or disreputable characters."

The reason for the warning was clear—gambling would play a central role at the racetrack. That meant a special effort by promoters to make sure visitors knew that crookedness was not to be tolerated, although there was a sense in later years that the sanctimonious message was delivered with a wink and a nod. Promoters told newspapermen that nothing in Virginia law prevented racing and "pool selling." The recently enacted Mushback law—as it was known because of its chief sponsor, Virginia Senator George Mushback—was aimed at the riffraff that congregated at Jackson City.

"The law, however, provides that pools may be sold on regular race tracks and on fairgrounds," the *Washington Post* reported. "This, it would seem, legalizes the St. Asaph scheme."

The scheme worked like this—all bets were officially made in Harper's Ferry at the so-called West Virginia Athletic Association, a dummy corporation set up to skirt Virginia law. All transactions were conducted by another sham operation, the Old Dominion Telegraph. To get around the liquor law, racetrack leaders created the Hiawatha Pleasure and Social Club. Printed on the back of every ticket was a vigorous statement denying that the operation is in any sense a poolroom.

Perhaps the most important part of the racetrack was the high-tech nature of the operation—especially for the 1890s. A telegraph office was located beneath the grandstand, with wires running into all the leading centers of the United States. It employed about forty bookmakers in a glass-enclosed nerve center, keeping the inclement weather out as the machines and bookies hummed with action.

By 1895, the Hills were ready to call a truce with the Jones family. Early in the year, the two warring clans reached an agreement. The two families would race on alternative days at their tracks, Jackson City one day and St. Asaph the next. The newfound family coalition didn't end there. When members of the General Assembly gathered in Richmond the following January, many legislators wanted to outlaw gambling once and for all.

But the Jones-Hill syndicate had other plans. They worked with their friends in the General Assembly to sneak yet another loophole into the law, this one more hidden than the last. The title of the bill was phrased in a way that was intentionally defective. That way, when lawyers representing Jones and Hill appeared in court, they could argue—rightfully—that the law was unconstitutional because the title was not sufficient to cover the contents.

The Hills returned to their operation at St. Asaph, and the Joneses kept up theirs at Jackson City. Then, in the winter of 1896, the two families staged a merger. The Hills took the Joneses in with them at St. Asaph. In combination, the former rival families flourished. They certainly were able to exercise power in Richmond, preventing several anti-gambling bills from ever seeing the light of day.

During the Spanish-American War, the United States government leased the St. Asaph property and used it as a quartermaster's supply depot and corral. But after the war, the track flourished like never before. By 1905, the gambling operation employed thirty-seven people—one for every house then standing in Del Ray.

Although it was wildly successful, the operation also had a dark side. Like the Sunday bars in Rosslyn and the ramshackle casinos of Jackson City, the St. Asaph Racetrack attracted a violent sort. Contemporaneous reports show farmers and even schoolchildren attacked as they were traveling between Alexandria County and the District of Columbia, mugged for cash that could then be gambled away.

Many readers were shocked to read in the *Alexandria Gazette* about shameful activities at the track, including forcing some of the horses to wear lead shoes to slow them down and skew the races. Some readers may have experienced a bit of cognitive dissonance when the same newspaper carried advertisements for "Racing Every Monday, Wednesday and Friday Until Further Notice—Objectionable Characters Will Be Positively Excluded."

One of the most prominent activists leading the charge against the racetrack was Joseph Suplee, who moved to Del Ray in 1895. He helped circulate a petition against the racetrack during the next legislative session in Richmond. Ministers and businessmen headed mass meetings calling attention to the scourge of racing, gambling and their associated violence.

Suplee was quoted as "defying anyone to prove the race track had brought any dollars into the community…it kept away good, law-abiding citizens." If the track were gone, Suplee said, the country between Alexandria city and Alexandria County would be built up immediately and "thus bring a more actual pecuniary benefit than the race tracks could ever accomplish."

When the effort was considered in committee, however, vestiges of the Old South stood in the way of progress for Suplee and other reformers. Horse racing was a time-honored Virginia pastime, after all. And members of the General Assembly were not about to come out against a good horse race, although that didn't mean that they were necessarily against gambling.

Ultimately, the lawmakers decided to do nothing.

RAID!

The posse of six men met on a Sunday in May and boarded the Alexandria and Mount Vernon Railroad southbound across the Long Bridge. Once the streetcar was in motion, Crandal Mackey dumped several sacks in the aisle full of axes, guns and sledgehammers—the weapons of progress. As arranged, the conductor made a special stop. The raid was on.

Exiting the streetcar, the posse found a high board fence around its first target, a place the *Evening Star* described as a "building in which all kinds of games were in the habit of being conducted." Fortunately for the armed posse, unsuspecting gamblers had left the gate open. According to the *Star*'s eyewitness account of the raid, the gamblers all "suddenly recalled that they had engagements."

The mad dash for the exits must have been chaotic. "It did not bother them whether they left through the open doors or the closed windows," the *Star* reported.

But the raiders were disappointed. A thorough search of the place failed to uncover any bookmaking. Instead, the men ended up busting a poker game. So the posse headed for Heath's Place, the infamous gambling establishment on the banks of the Potomac River opposite Georgetown University. There they were confronted by Eddie Heath, proprietor of the infamous hillside gambling parlor. Heath stood at the door with a double-barrel shotgun, threatening to kill the first man who tried to enter.

Mackey rushed up and disarmed him, and then his deputies hauled him off to jail. For the raiding party, it was a long-awaited moment of revenge.

The plaque attached to Crandal Mackey's shotgun. *Brandy Crist-Travers.*

Six years earlier, Heath's place had been raided by six members of the Good Citizens League. One of the raiders, thirty-nine-year-old Lemuel Marcey, was felled by a club and beaten unconscious with a pistol butt. Now, more than half a decade later, he was out for revenge—acting as one of the ringleaders in Mackey's posse and swearing-in the volunteers as official deputies of Alexandria County.

When members of the raiding party headed downstairs, they found poker tables and a bar. Upstairs, the men found the faro bank, the craps table, the hazard board and the keno tables. The deputized men in the raiding party then hacked up the bars, drained bottles of "ardent spirits," destroyed the slot machines, wrecked a policy wheel and, of course, gathered evidence. In the chaos, someone toppled a music box that began to play "There'll Be a Hot Time in the Old Town Tonight."

Unfortunately for Mackey, the raiding party found only one or two employees and two or three patrons. Only a few tables were in operation. Newspapers speculated that Sheriff William Palmer may have tipped Heath off to the raid.

"The statement that Heath had been tipped off by a member of my staff is absolutely false," Palmer responded to a reporter for the *Washington Post*. "First for the reason that no one, not even the deputies in question knew of the

Heath's Place was a notorious spot in the woods near Rosslyn. *Virginia Room, Arlington Public Library.*

contemplated raid, and second…that it had been known that a raid was to be made, the games would not have been in progress."

Whether or not that was the case, much of his gaming paraphernalia was not around when the raid went down. Apparently, he had stashed his devices in Washington—far from the long arm of the law and waiting for a day when it would be safe on the other side of the Potomac River once again. A few token items were confiscated, and Heath was arrested along with two of his employees.

"I am not advised as to whether or not any gambling paraphernalia had been removed to Washington," said Sheriff Palmer. "I would say, however, that it would have been advisable to do so owing to the proximity of the premises to the residence of the commonwealth's attorney."

From Heath's place, the posse moved south to Jackson City, the infamous hellhole on the Virginia side of the Long Bridge. When the men arrived, one of the deputies caused some uneasiness when he discharged his revolver to frighten a fleeing black man.

The *Washington Times* promoted Crandal Mackey's crusade with frequent stories, including this feature from May 22, 1904. *Library of Congress.*

"Some of those in the party were anxious to apply the torch," the *Star* reported, "but Mackey would not countenance such conduct."

Instead, the commonwealth's attorney oversaw a path of destruction. "They cut down the paintings, hacked the walls, broke the chairs and all the beautiful furniture, the tables, everything," recalled Frank Ball. "They just cut it into pieces."

In the end, the posse "made a demonstration which is intended to give the lawbreakers an idea of what they may expect if they persist," the *Star* reported. From there, the deputies set their sights on an infamous saloon operated by Jimmy Lafontaine at the south end of the Long Bridge. Lafontaine was arrested along with two associates, Charles Sanderson and Pat Ready.

"It is contended by Lafontaine and his two associates that Ready was cleaning up the bar at the time of the raid, and there was no gaming going on," the *Washington Times* reported.

The raids made Mackey an instant celebrity. His face was plastered across newspaper inches, and his name became synonymous with cleaning up crime and corruption. He was an instant legend or villain, depending on your point of view. For the reform set, he was a white knight in shining armor. For the corrupt politicians and saloon managers, he was the devil incarnate.

"I will close them," he bragged to the *Washington Post*, "even if I have to ask the governor to station a squad of soldiers in every gambling resort in the county."

Dealing with the St. Asaph Racetrack was more difficult. Before he even attempted a raid on the racetrack, he wanted to lay the groundwork first. That meant exposing the insider's game that was being played at St. Asaph.

"The gambling ring is a bigger thing than many people believe," Mackey told the *Washington Post*. "The St. Asaph ring has been a power so potent in Virginia and particularly in Alexandria County that for years every one of the 22 delegates from the county in a gubernatorial convention has voted for their candidate."

Mackey went on to explain that some backers of the poolroom don't go near the place for weeks or months at a time, but he knew almost all of them anyway. "I believe I can lay my hands on people who can and will give the kind of testimony I want at the proper time," Mackey boasted.

Mackey knew that conducting a raid on St. Asaph would require more foresight than simply showing up with an axe-wielding posse. To gain an exclusive indictment against the St. Asaph Racetrack, Mackey released the grand jury to place its own bets and gather firsthand evidence. The day after the raid on Rosslyn and Jackson City, Mackey issued nineteen warrants for men believed to be responsible for bookmaking and gaming at St. Asaph's racetrack. Charges were filed against some of the leading members of the Jones-Hill syndicate that ran the infamous poolrooms.

"It is understood that the Hills will make no resistance but will agree to arrest," the *Washington Times* reported. "It is also rumored that they have employed some of the best legal talent in Washington, Baltimore and Richmond, Va., to represent them at the trials."

When all the smoke cleared, only six men were arrested—a disappointingly small outcome for such a well-orchestrated dragnet effort. Speculated mounted that Sheriff Palmer may have been working against the effort, tipping off the gambling interests and undercutting the success of the raids. All six were taken before a justice of the peace and released on bail to appear in the court the following Wednesday.

After the raids, tension began to build between Mackey and Palmer. According to news accounts, the prosecutor was angry with the sheriff for serving the warrants on the poolroom operators at St. Asaph without arresting any of the men he found there.

"The lawyer remarks that either the sheriff does not know his duty, or else he does not care to perform it," the *Washington Times* reported.

From that point on, Mackey announced, he would be serving warrants himself. The arrangement was not unprecedented, and newspapers compared the situation in Alexandria County to William Travers Jerome of New York, a prosecutor who also served his own warrants. Palmer, meanwhile, was compared to the infamously crooked New York City police chief William Stephen Devery.

"Certainly this looks as if Alexandria County were assuming a real metropolitan aspect, while Sheriff Palmer is certainly getting in line to compare notes with Big Chief Bill Devery when they meet on the other side of the great divide," the *Washington Times* noted.

By the middle of May, the legal fight had begun to take shape. Justice of the Peace Patrick Hagan issued warrants against eighteen men. They were charged with violating the anti-gambling laws of Virginia. The men immediately put together a stellar legal team, including the same legal lawyers who fought Mackey when he was first elected. The legal trio went on the offensive. Appearing in Alexandria County Court, the lawyers said that Justice Hagan should be prohibited from the case because he had not qualified by taking the oath of office and giving bond. They also attacked irregularities in the warrants and charged that the campaign against their clients was unconstitutional.

This antique slot machine is similar to the ones used in Rosslyn and Jackson City. *Library of Congress.*

"The gamblers have money and will spend it," the *Washington Times* reported. "Mackey has brains and nerve and, so far, he has proven equal to the occasion."

Strangely, the *Alexandria Gazette* engaged in selective reporting of the raid on the racetrack. The May 20, 1904 issue carried a one-paragraph notice under the headline "Wires Cut Out." Amazingly, the paragraph made no mention of the newly elected commonwealth's attorney or his crusade against gambling and corruption. It was a curious way to report events, especially considering all the ink thrown at Crandal Mackey by the *Times*, the *Star* and the *Post*.

"Wires and telegraph instruments of the Western Union company were removed from the St. Asaph poolroom yesterday," the *Gazette* reported. "The poolroom employees stated that they would have satisfactory arrangements for handling returns completed in a few days, but what their plans are they declined to disclose."

The *Gazette* reported that the poolroom will have agents of its own at all the tracks who would be filing race results at telegraph stations nearest their respective tracks. Those returns would be received at the nearest office to St.

Asaph. Because it was a common carrier, the *Gazette* reported, it would have to handle this business.

"Receiving returns in this manner will necessitate a string of messenger boys from the telegraph office to the poolroom, and the results cannot be made known so quickly as heretofore," the *Gazette* explained. "It is not known how soon these arrangement can be perfected."

It was clear that powerful and unseen forces were at work. In the courtroom, the legal team for the racetrack sought to gain a writ of prohibition—essentially shutting down the prosecution—and they were successful. On May 12, Judge Charles Nicol granted the writ. This was a strategy that was used over and over again against Mackey, with mixed results. For now, at least, gaining the writ of prohibition was able to kick the can down the road and postpone the case until at least June. Despite Nicol's ruling, Mackey told the *Washington Post* that the judge was one of the "cleanest men and foremost jurists of Virginia, who has no superior at the bar."

By the end of May, gambling was lively again in Northern Virginia. Rosslyn may have been quieted, and the Western Union lines at St. Asaph may have gone dead, but the Long Bridge Monte Carlo would not die. The *Washington Times* reported that Jackson City was already going "at full blast." Sweatboards and policy and crap games were being conducted by some of the same men who were raided only a few days before. Apparently, they feared nothing from the long arm of the law.

Meanwhile, the proprietors of the St. Asaph poolroom were in New York attending a conference of poolroom operators from around the country and trying to figure out how to reopen their operation. Many assumed that it wouldn't be long before the "Old Dominion Telegraph Company" was doing business once again at the same stand, as well as once again forwarding commissions to the "West Virginia Athletic Association." Some speculated that a new poolroom would open in Rosslyn.

The raids may have transformed Crandal Mackey into a cult figure, but that didn't mean he was finished. Not by a long shot.

Fighting St. Asaph

The fight against St. Asaph wasn't just about gambling. It was also about corruption.

Crandal Mackey's raids in Rosslyn and Jackson City went off largely without a hitch, except for some hesitation on the part of the sheriff. For the most part, the card sharks and saloon managers scampered like roaches when the prosecutor showed up with a shotgun.

Not so at St. Asaph. The racetrack was popular, and it brought in thousands of dollars in revenue each day it was open. Perhaps even more importantly, the investors who created the joint were the insiders' insiders. The list of original 1894 investors reads like a city directory of power and money: John Marriott Hill, William Daingerfield, George Uhler and Park Agnew. But one man towered above the rest: Virginia Senator George Mushback.

A former city councilman, Mushback represented Alexandria in the House of Delegates before moving on to the Virginia state Senate. By the mid-1890s, he had achieved a kind of legendary status in Richmond, a large man with an imposing sense of power and influence on the Appropriations Committee. His passport application notes that he had blue-gray eyes and a medium complexion, with an oval face, a medium-high forehead and curly gray-brown hair. He wore a mustache, as did many men in that era, and had a slight cleft chin.

In the Senate, Mushback passed legislation that benefited himself. Specifically, he was responsible for several pieces of anti-gambling legislation—ones in which he conveniently created loopholes to give

This cartoon was published on the front page of the *Washington Times* on January 13, 1905. *Virginia Room, Arlington Public Library.*

the gentleman's club a competitive advantage over its more ramshackle competitors. Gamblers knew that they could have a dangerous game of poker in Rosslyn, but they might end up in Dead Man's Hollow. And they could play a game of policy in Jackson City, but they might get stabbed on Long Bridge.

St. Asaph was high class and connected. Originally known as the Gentleman's Driving Park at the St. Asaph Junction, the operation eventually became known as the St. Asaph Racetrack. And Mushback used the levers of power to protect it. His legislation was riddled with exemptions that could be used for certain kinds of associations, including the driving club he set up with his friends from Alexandria City Hall. He worked the system like a pro.

During the 1896 session, when anti-gambling sentiment was reaching a fever pitch, Delegate Addison Maupin of Henrico wanted to close a loophole that allowed agricultural societies to operate gambling establishments. Mushback used the opportunity as a way to hide even more exemptions within the legislation, ensuring that St. Asaph remained the gambling capital of Northern Virginia. "As a lawyer, he was eminently successful," gushed the *Richmond Times* obituary five years later.

After Mushback's death, however, things changed. The racetrack no longer had the chairman of the Senate Appropriations Committee to watch its back. Now it had Commonwealth's Attorney Crandal Mackey and his shotgun to deal with. But Mackey didn't use the shotgun. Instead, he issued a series of warrants against the Jones-Hill syndicate, the formerly warring families who had combined forces to rule the territory.

To persuade the grand jury, Mackey took the members on a field trip to St. Asaph, where they put down a number of bets. Then they returned to the courthouse and heard Mackey read from a statute against betting on "baseball, football, or the trial of speed or power of endurance of any animal or beast."

"The difficulties of the situation are, however, more political than legal," the *Washington Times* noted.

Unsurprisingly, the syndicate put together a stellar legal team—the same trio of lawyers that contested Mackey's razor-thin election a few months earlier. Leading the charge was banker Edmund Burke, the great-great-grandson of Thomas Jefferson and founder of Alexandria's oldest bank. Then there was Francis Smith, the hard-charging chairman of the school board and longtime legal partner to Senator George Mushback. Joining the team as the junior partner was Charles Creighton Carlin, a thirty-eight-year-old notary public who would later to go on to represent Alexandria in

Congress. The *Washington Times* described them as "shrewd and able lawyers, several of whom have political influence enough to make them formidable under certain conditions."

The list of warrants Crandal Mackey served that cold May morning included a special officer of Alexandria County. He and five justices of the peace were later removed from office. Many on the hit list were members of the Hill family and the Jones family. These were people who were ready, willing and able to protect their interests. The *Washington Times* suggested that the Jones-Hill syndicate could control as much as $1 million, an unbelievable amount of money for the era.

"That they have spent money like water and will do so again, none will deny," the *Washington Times* reported. "The only trouble lies in the as yet unanswered question—Will their money do them any good in the present contest?"

The ramifications of the arrest warrants were far-reaching, and the profits were spread among many. It's possible that Crandal Mackey did not even fully realize the extent of who was behind the St. Asaph Racetrack. As the court case moved forward in the courtroom of Judge Charles Nicol, more would be revealed about the powerful forces behind the St. Asaph Racetrack. For now, though, the fight was among the team of superb lawyers and the newly elected prosecutor with a reputation for resisting the powerful political machine.

"Crandal Mackey they know to be honest," the *Times* reported. "Efforts have been made, it is said, to fix Mackey through his friends. They have failed."

Mackey's salary as commonwealth's attorney was only $300 per year, not nearly enough to make him a player on the field of business. In some ways, his salary was tied to the kind of prosecution that would make him infamous. For each gambling or revenue case or felony, he was given $10. For each misdemeanor, he was given $5.

"If Mackey is honest; if Mackey has nerve; if Mackey has brains he can do it," proclaimed one anonymous source to the *Washington Times*. "The gamblers have money and nerve. The lawyers have employed the brains, and the combination will fight to the last ditch."

The aim of the St. Asaph legal team was to stall, creating a long and drawn-out legal battle in which every move and countermove would be thoroughly scrutinized. Once the team appealed the accusations beyond Judge Charles Nicol, according to its strategy, the problem would go away and it could start making money again. The case would be in an endless legal limbo, as appeal after appeal kept the accusations deadlocked indefinitely. Meanwhile, the Western Union lines would keep humming along.

The case was scheduled for the courtroom of Judge Nicol, who was also the president of the Alexandria National Bank. The *Washington Times* seemed to have confidence that "all the gamblers and all the politicians in Virginia would not cause him the tremor of an eyelid." Like the progressive victory over the machine in the 1901 race for governor, a change was moving across Alexandria. Letters of support were pouring into Mackey's office, and newspapers such as the *Washington Times* were on board with the fight, even if the *Alexandria Gazette* was not. The prosecutor was even receiving countless offers from supporters who wanted to act as deputies in future raids.

But Mackey had a difficult fight on his hands. The opposing legal team was out for blood, and the men were eager to catch the young prosecutor napping. At one point, they sought a delay because the justice of the peace who issued the warrants had not taken the oath of office or given bond. At another point, the lawyers for the gamblers sought a delay when Mackey failed to bring original papers to the courtroom. The legal eagles were clearly running circles around Mackey, who was encouraged by some of his supporters to drop the case against St. Asaph.

"I have no intention of resigning or of giving up the fight," Mackey told the *Washington Times*. "I burned my bridges behind me when I took up this fight, and I am going to push it for all I am worth."

Encouraged by his success in Rosslyn and at Jackson City, Mackey wanted to finish the job. Putting the most infamous gambling resort in Northern Virginia out of business for good was the only way to fulfill his campaign promise. The prosecution eventually became a crusade as St. Crandal fought back a series of legal demons out of the apocalyptic legal volumes the opposing counsel wielded as weapons.

"All the other gambling resorts in Alexandria County are out of business, and St. Asaph will follow before long," proclaimed Mackey. "If there is law enough on the Virginia statute books for the purpose I am going to close the St. Asaph poolroom."

During one hearing at Manassas, Mackey was caught napping again. Attorneys for the gamblers asked the judge to dismiss the case because they identified "James M. Hill," not John Marriott Hill. Mackey asked to have the case heard anyway. "They are quibbling," Mackey told Judge Nicol. "All they want, your honor, is to delay the trial of these cases so the racetrack people can run their gambling game and make money enough to pay counsel fees."

But Nicol said that he had no other option than to sustain the objection, granting yet another delay. It was an embarrassing moment for Mackey, and several newspapers said that the newly elected prosecutor had been trumped.

"Sooner or later this case will come before the courts and be decided on its merits," Mackey responded. "Then we will see who wins out."

By the middle of June 1904, momentum seemed to shift. The racetrack had closed after Western Union abolished its "information bureau," cutting service to poolrooms throughout the country. Gamblers who kept showing up on the "race special" of the Washington, Alexandria and Mount Vernon Electric Railway arrived to learn that there was "nothin' doin'" at the track. John Marriott Hill told the *Washington Times* that he hoped to reopen the track as soon as possible, and he seemed confident that the gamblers would prevail in court.

"The truth of the matter is that we have nothing to conceal about our pool room," John Marriott Hill told the *Washington Times*. "We are running within the requirements of the law and have always done so."

Mackey's strategy was patience. He knew that the opposition would try every trick in the book to delay the proceedings and drag out the legal process. Like the proverbial tortoise racing against the hare, Mackey felt confident that time was on his side. And he was willing to wait for victory.

"The fight against St. Asaph has just begun," Mackey told the *Washington Times* in June. "This case is bound to come to an issue some time. When it is heard on its merits, there will be a different tune sung."

It wasn't long before the Western Union line had been restored and the racetrack was back in operation as the poolroom buzzed with activity. During the few days the track was closed, similar operations outside Baltimore profited temporarily. But the Hill brothers left no stone unturned in their efforts to reopen St. Asaph. By the time the thoroughbreds were thundering around the Sheepshead course, the crowds were back in force.

"Betting was lively," reported the *Washington Times*. "But a keen lookout was kept for any of Mackey's deputies who might be wandering around loose."

The confrontation finally happened on Thursday, June 20, 1904. Attorneys for both sides arrived at the red brick courthouse in carriages packed with legal volumes, loaded for bear. One journalist described the mood as upbeat, as the lawyers chatted amiably and waited for the proceedings to begin. Francis Smith and C.C. Carlin arrived early. Edmund Burke strolled in late, making a striking appearance in immaculate white duck pants and patent leather shoes. The portly lawyer wore a dotted white shirt, a dark coat, a blue necktie and a small diamond stud glistened in the field of black and white.

After the judge gaveled the session into order, Mackey launched into a full-throated attack on the racetrack. He began by describing a pool-betting operation in detail.

"Isn't that right, Mr. Burke," Mackey asked, turning toward the elder statesman of the opposing legal side.

"I never went into a pool in my life," Burke responded. "I never went into the small ones, and I never had money enough to go into the large ones."

"Let us hope you will have money enough some day," Carlin added.

"Maybe I will when I get my fee," Burke concluded.

Each side had three hours to argue the case. Mackey said he felt that the law on the Virginia statute books was against the conduct of gambling houses in Alexandria. He described Alexandria County has a "sinkhole" and an "asylum for gamblers." Then the prosecutor reviewed the last decade of General Assembly action against gambling, prompting repeated wrangling from opposing counsel. In the end, little was accomplished that day in court. The judge ended up making a technical ruling about a demurrer that Mackey filed to the petition for a writ of prohibition.

"The impression among other lawyers around the courthouse was that they would never let the merits of the case be tried if they could possibly prevent it," the *Washington Times* reported. "It is likely that from now to a time far distant the intellects of Mackey and his opponents will grapple with many intricate legal problem before they get to a point where the court can pass upon the law in the case."

That case eventually fizzled, but Mackey was not done. In September, the prosecutor was back on the attack. On September 13, 1904, he sent five warrants to Sheriff William Palmer for the arrest of John Marriott Hill, Frank Hill, Zora Hill, Louise Bargen and Charles Burlingame. The Hill brothers all held a direct interest in the St. Asaph poolroom, and Burlingame was the telegraph operator.

Mackey directed Palmer to close St. Asaph and arrest the men on charges of running a gambling establishment contrary to the laws of Virginia. A hearing was set before Justice of the Peace Josiah Haney of the Jefferson magisterial district at the Del Ray schoolhouse. But when the court date arrived, Haney announced that he felt incompetent to try the case alone because the case was an important one "involving not only a large amount of money, but the honor and fair fame of Alexandria County as well." So he called two other justices to sit with him.

"Before we have gone too far, a legal fog will arise and the contest will become strenuous," Haney explained. "Therefore I have called to my assistance two other justices."

Mackey objected, refusing to have the additional justices added to the bench and imploring Haney to do his duty. He reminded the judge that a previous hearing in the case determined that only the justice of the magisterial district where the alleged crimes occurred could try the proprietors of the poolroom, as well as that Haney was the justice for the Jefferson District and should, therefore, perform his duties. One journalist who witnessed the hearing at the Del Ray schoolhouse described Haney as "visibly nervous, his hands trembling as he rose to speak."

"I will not change my position in regard to having Justices East and Jones sit with me, unless you show me the law that compels me to," said Haney. "I assure you all justice in this case."

Mackey knew that Jones had already expressed an opinion that the St. Asaph poolroom business was legal, so the situation was fraught with danger. And East was a justice of the peace in a different magisterial district who had caused a previous case to fall apart. Mackey asked for a few minutes with the grand jury, the same group of men that visited St. Asaph in the spring to obtain evidence. After a brief consultation, the prosecutor addressed the court. "It is the unanimous view of the grand jury that it would be unwise for me to go on with the case under the present circumstances," Mackey explained. "I decline, therefore, to prosecute on these warrants."

The announcement struck like a thunderclap. Here was the prosecutor who had put St. Asaph at the center of his efforts to clean up Alexandria County withdrawing his case. Almost immediately, attorneys for the gamblers went into a huddle and determined their next court of action. Within a few minutes, Burke complained of the expense of bringing witnesses from Pennsylvania and West Virginia. He said that he didn't understand Mackey's concerns and asked Haney to continue.

Burke said that it would be hardship on his clients if they were not acquitted of the charge, as well as that the case shouldn't be thrown out just because Mackey withdrew the case. Haney said that he wanted to confer with the other two justices. "We want to ask each other a few questions," he said.

Then the three justices retired to the schoolyard. When they returned, Haney had an announcement to make. "We unanimously agree that the defendants are acquitted of the charge contained in these warrants," said the justice.

It was a body blow to Mackey and his ten-month effort to shut down St. Asaph, one that must have been terribly frustrating to the prosecutor. A few days after the acquittal, Mackey issued a written statement explaining that he "would not be surprised from the talk I have heard to see a vigilance committee organize to close the St. Asaph poolroom." The muckraking *Washington Times* was not impressed.

"So far, the result of the fight on the poolrooms at St. Asaph is a complete failure," wrote editors of the *Times* in a scathing editorial. "Mr. Mackey might just as well never have been elected."

The *Times* chastised Mackey for a number of shortcomings: failing to bring original papers to court, including wrong names on court documents and, ultimately, abandoning his own case against the St. Asaph proprietors. The editorial suggested that the law officers in Alexandria must be either incompetent or corrupt, although it challenged Mackey to prove it in court rather than making charges in the press.

"He must act, and act vigorously," the *Times* editorialized. "If he continues trying cases against determined men as though pleading in a moot court, he will rightly lose all the standing he now possesses."

The next month, Mackey was back in the fight, serving yet another warrant on John Marriott Hill. Once again, Mackey called on Justice of the Peace Josiah Haney, who had jurisdiction over the Jefferson magisterial district where the poolroom was located, to hear the charge against Hill of operating a racetrack gambling establishment contrary to the laws of Virginia. Many people were starting to question whether this young prosecutor had what it took to take on the powerful Hill family and all the money associated with the gambling industry.

"Hill is a very popular man personally, and his friends stick by him closer than Mackey's do by him," the *Washington Times* reported. "Also, he has abundant means at his command, and has procured the services of good lawyers."

Those lawyers went to work using the familiar tactics of delay and obstruction. They persuaded the court of appeals to order the justice of the peace to suspend all proceedings until a writ of prohibition could be heard in Richmond in November. The basis for that action was that St. Asaph was within a mile of Alexandria city, a suggestion that the operation fell under the exclusive jurisdiction of the Police Court in Alexandria. The stakes were high because if the court agreed, that would mean that Crandal Mackey had no jurisdiction over St. Asaph.

"The St. Asaph proprietors have always contended that they are conducting a legal business," the *Alexandria Gazette* editorialized. "From the manner in which they have resisted in the court's every effort to interfere with them, it would seem that they are sincere in their belief."

The strategy of the gambling team was clear: assert the city's jurisdiction over St. Asaph and push Crandal Mackey out of the picture. The writ of prohibition sought to have Alexandria City Hall take over the case and vanquish the crusading county prosecutor. Because the operation was within a mile of the city, the logic went, city officials had exclusive jurisdiction—even if St. Asaph was technically in the Jefferson District of Alexandria County.

"If the writ is sustained by the court of appeals, Crandal Mackey, commonwealth's attorney for Alexandria County, will have no more to do with the case," the *Washington Times* explained. "It will be up to the commonwealth's attorney of Alexandria City, Samuel Brent, and Mayor Paff to attempt to break up the poolroom or let it alone, as they see fit."

The fix was in. Or at least that's what the attorneys for the gamblers thought. Leaders at Alexandria City Hall were working behind the scenes with the Hill brothers to find some way of getting rid of Mackey. Over the next few months, they put together a plan to stage a fake raid in an effort to put some closure on the long and drawn-out prosecution.

It was a gamble, but this was a crowd that was used to a gamble. The idea was to have Alexandria City Commonwealth's Attorney S.G. Brent present weak evidence and gain a court victory. If they were unable to get a judge in on their scheme, Mackey later explained, the attorneys planned on appealing the case and entering false evidence into the record that would be able to exonerate their operation. At the center of the scheme was proving in court that the betting at St. Asaph was done on the lands of a gentlemen's driving park—capitalizing on the late Senator George Mushback's legislation intended to give the operation a competitive advantage.

By January, all the pieces of the conspiracy had been set in place. The Hill brothers and the city leaders were ready to stage the bogus raid. There was only one small problem. On the day of the fraudulent police action, John Marriott Hill was delayed by a trolley accident. Unwilling to let the ruse move forward without his personal oversight, Hill sent word by telephone that the operation should be delayed.

"Mr. Hill is detained by a trolley accident," according to the telephone message. "Do not do anything until he gets there."

Unfortunately for Hill, the message did not reach Alexandria City Hall. Instead, by some bizarre fluke, the message was routed to the Alexandria County Courthouse, and it went straight to Mackey. Meanwhile, at Alexandria City Hall, Mayor Frederick Paff hit the roof. It seems that in all the planning for the fraud, nobody bothered to tell the mayor that the Alexandria Police Department was planning a raid outside the city limits.

"The whole thing was carried on without my knowledge or consent," Paff told the press. "I think that Alexandria has enough to do to look after what goes on within her borders without going into Alexandria County."

Finally, Mackey had his big break. The mayor was apoplectic. The Hill brothers had unintentionally exposed themselves. And the dream team of lawyers would not be able to delay their way out of this one. Mackey summoned reporters to his office on a brisk January morning and unveiled the fraud, which was splashed across the front page of the *Washington Times* that afternoon.

"The whole thing was a fake, not only expected but planned by Hill and his associates," Mackey told the *Times*. "I know that Attorney Brent has no evidence on which he can convict the accused, and unless I am very much mistaken, what evidence is brought out by him at the trial will have been furnished him by the gamblers themselves." Finally, after more than a year, Mackey had achieved victory.

Within hours of the *Washington Times* exposing their fraud on the front page, attorneys for the gamblers began negotiating with the commonwealth's attorney for Alexandria County. In a series of closed-door meetings, the prosecutors and the defense attorneys negotiated a deal. If the racetrack were to close its doors, according to the bargain, Mackey would drop all prosecution. As an insurance policy, Mackey said that he would suspend the case rather than withdraw it, just in case the gamblers decided to open up shop again. The headline and subhead in the *Times* the following day said it all: "Poolroom at St. Asaph Promises to Move Away: Commonwealth Attorney Mackey Wins Fight to Drive Gamblers from Alexandria County— Allows Case Continued."

Later that month, the residents of the St. Elmo and Del Ray neighborhoods in the Jefferson District of Alexandria County celebrated Mackey with a banquet in honor of his victory against the St. Asaph poolroom. The celebration was held at the Del Ray schoolhouse, a stone's throw from the now-shuttered gambling operation. Former Alexandria Mayor George Simpson and Alexandria County *Monitor* editor Frank Lyons were the principal speakers.

"Mr. Mackey was introduced by George Garrett, chairman of the meeting," the *Washington Times* reported. "Mr. Garrett humorously remarked that Mr. Mackey would be expected to give a lecture upon the best method of making a graft on a plum tree."

MUCKRAKING PROSECUTOR

Crandal Mackey took office on a chilly Monday in 1904. Walking into his office at the courthouse that morning, the newly elected commonwealth's attorney found himself in a world of political corruption, vice and crime. The first prosecution was a gruesome murder case involving a black man named John Williams, who was indicted for the murder of Joseph Johnson, another black man, back in November. According to news accounts, when the case was submitted to the jury for decision, Williams called out to his attorney.

"Well," he said, according to an account in the *Washington Times*, "I guess they'll send me up the road."

"Why if you are found guilty of murder in the first degree," his lawyer responded, "you will be hanged."

"That will be bad for me," Williams replied. "Will they hang me tonight if they say I'm guilty?"

The lawyer assured him that he would not be executed that evening, and the *Times* reported that Williams seemed satisfied with that. He was eventually found guilty of second-degree murder, narrowly escaping the death penalty. It was an important lesson for the newly elected commonwealth's attorney about how justice is perceived from opposite sides of the courtroom. Justice is swift, but it's never that swift.

With that in mind, Mackey turned back to his signature issue—going after the gambling interests. It was a crusade that he would relish for the rest of his life, including a mention of himself in his history of the county.

Commonwealth's Attorney Crandal Mackey walks along Long Bridge near Jackson City.
Virginia Room, Arlington Public Library.

"In 1905, the writer caused the arrest of persons who were running a pool room for race track gambling at Jackson City," Mackey wrote in his book tracing the history of Alexandria County.

The raid against Jackson City was not the end of the story, not by a long shot. Proprietors tried to argue in federal court that they were beyond the long arm of the law in Virginia. The team of lawyers was attempting to capitalize on potential legal ambiguity dating back to retrocession, the 1847 act of the Virginia General Assembly asserting its claim to land that had been part of the original District of Columbia. Appearing before a judge in the Eastern District of Virginia, the lawyers tried to make the case that Jackson City was in the District of Columbia, not Virginia. Therefore, according to the argument, officials in Virginia could not lawfully arrest or try them.

At a hearing in Richmond, Mackey argued that the judge should dismiss the petition on the grounds that an individual could not raise the question of the validity of retrocession. Even if they could, Mackey argued, they should have applied to the Supreme Court of the District of Columbia for their writs of habeas corpus. The argument was then—and now—somewhat of a legal gray area.

Back in 1875, a large property owner in Alexandria County by the name of Robert Phillips tried to get out of paying his taxes by arguing that Virginia had no legal authority to send him a tax bill. The argument was that retrocession was unconstitutional and therefore Virginia had no legal claim to property in Alexandria County. The lawsuit was aimed at Charles Payne, collector of taxes of Washington District in Alexandria County, to recover $165 in taxes.

"On April 17, 1876, the Supreme Court of the United States decided the case by most adroitly and artfully dodging the real question involved," Mackey wrote in his history of the county.

Under Chief Justice Morrison Waite, the court sidestepped the issue of whether or not retrocession was constitutional. Instead, the justices merely said that Phillips had no standing to bring the case. Of course, that left the issue unresolved. Massachusetts Senator George Frisbie Hoar introduced a bill authorizing the attorney general to bring a suit to test the constitutionality of retrocession, but the matter died in committee.

"Since this decision the question of ceding back the county of Alexandria to the United States has been agitated in public meetings in the county, and frequently in Congress," Mackey wrote.

This was the legal ambiguity that the lawyers representing Jackson City gamblers were betting would save the day. They lost the bet. The judge dismissed their motion, and the infamous gambling houses of Jackson City shut their doors—although this would not be the last of the infamous gambling houses named for Old Hickory.

Not all of Mackey's cases were quite so earth shattering. In the summer of 1906, he went after nude bathers. For many years, the Virginia side of the Potomac River attracted in-the-buff swimming by small boys and half-grown men. Mackey responded by posting a deputy in plain clothes to patrol that side of the river. On a more serious note, he also began talking about furnishing a library for the public schools. He became a trustee of Arlington National Bank. And he was listed as a vice-president of the Alexandria-Washington Greater Highway Association. His star was clearly on the rise.

"He cleaned out that county in approved style, although it did take him some little time," declared Robert Peter, candidate for state's attorney in Rockville, Maryland. "Mackey stirred up public sentiment, got the people on his side, and then started out on a crusade."

It was clearly a template that Peter and others wanted to replicate. Mackey's single-minded determination to go after corrupt politicians and their loopholes was clearly catching on. "Games of chance are games of chance. It does not matter one whit whether they are indulged in or run by members of a club or organization," Peter declared on the campaign trail.

"The sandwich game doesn't go here. Whiskey is whiskey, and beer is beer, whether sold with a sandwich or by themselves."

In 1906, Crandal Mackey took on one of the most grueling prosecutions of his career—a case that dominated the headlines for months. It involved a black man by the name of Jackson Boney, who was found dead in a buggy on Long Bridge. Police initially arrested a black woman named Annie Green, who told several contradictory stories about her whereabouts that evening. But as it turns out, there was a highwayman who appeared on bridge and demanded money.

Boney just happened to be carrying $600 in cash, the result of a settlement agreement with the District government. Annie Green ended up picking the suspect out of a lineup of sixty or seventy prisoners, a man by the name of Joseph Wright. In court, Mackey painted Wright as a dangerous man who robbed Boney and raped Green. When Alexandria County residents found out about what had happened, many feared a lynch mob.

"There is no cause for a lynching," Mackey told the *Washington Times*. "If this man is guilty, we will convict him soon enough and the proper penalty will be inflicted."

In court, Mackey painted a picture of Wright as a vicious killer who held a club in his right hand and a pistol in the left. As Boney and Green were driving from Washington to Alexandria, Wright jumped out from behind a clump of bushes and fired one shot. Boney fell to the bottom of the buggy. Green shrieked, and Wright placed his hand on her mouth. Wright didn't take Boney's coins or his gold watch, but he did steal $600 in cold, hard cash.

"She identified him by his cross-eyes, by his flat nose, those thick, brutal lips, that neck and jaw, those round shoulders and that fiendish voice," the *Washington Times* reported. "He is a burly, brutal looking colored man, about five-feet, ten inches tall, and he has the most repulsive countenance. His eyes are defective, and he wears a silly grin on his face at all times."

The defense attorney was desperate for mercy. "This negro doesn't drink a drop of whiskey," he told the jury. "He can get it though. Maybe a negro who can get whiskey and doesn't get it ought to be hanged, but we're not trying that now."

Born in Loudoun County, Wright had always been somewhat of a shadowy figure. His parents were slaves, and defense attorneys dwelt at some length on the Civil War and its lasting consequences. None of that seemed to matter, though. Wright was sentenced to be "hanged until dead," an ignominious end to a difficult life.

"Residents of the county seem to be pretty well stirred up over the affair," Crandal Mackey told the *Washington Times*. "I have heard what the men intend to do, but I do not really believe that mob violence will be done."

The scaffolding was ordered at once. Workers constructed it ten feet from the ground, with a flight of winding steps leading upward. A crossbar made of heavy pine was painted a shade of dull brown. No more than twenty people could have fit in the enclosure, which was surrounded by a pine fence that was thirty feet high. As Wright whiled away the hours on Death Row, a Baptist preacher by the name of Mose visited him three or four times as the convict twanged merrily on an old banjo. Saws and hammer could be heard in the distance, constructing the final instrument of doom for Joseph Wright.

"His spiritual advisor says Wright will go to the scaffold with a firm step and iron nerve and swing into eternity with a protestation of innocence on his lips," reported the *Washington Times*.

Suddenly, without warning, politics stole the show. Claude Swanson had no love lost for Mackey, who campaigned against him for governor back in 1901. Swanson lost that race but apparently never forgot about the crusading progressive in Alexandria County. The lawyer from Danville was able to gain the upper hand the next election cycle, and it's clear that he had not forgotten the role that Mackey played in denying him the Governor's Mansion.

Governor Swanson commuted Wright's death sentence, sending him instead to life in prison. Mackey fought against the governor, but he was unable to change the course of events. Wright died in prison years later, and Mackey was denied the death sentence he so eagerly fought for in those early years of his term. The next few years were a blur of blood and gore. Murder, pestilence, crime and corruption. It was all in a day's work for Crandal Mackey, whose enemies were out for blood. By the time he was up for reelection, the machine wanted revenge.

"It is expected that the saloon element will line up with the sporting fraternity in an effort to secure Capt. Mackey's defeat," the *Washington Herald* reported. "A hard fight is expected in which outside influences will probably be brought to bolster up the campaign of the gambling element."

More than $2,500 was set aside to secure the election of an official favorable to the gambling interests, but the big poolrooms of St. Asaph remained closed. In late September, Charles Simms of Glencarlyn finally announced his candidacy against Mackey. He was running as a Republican, challenging Mackey, who was a Democrat running as an independent. But Simms had a serious problem. His reputation was against the gambling interests, and the *Washington Times* noted that Mackey and Simms stood for "practically the same reforms."

Rumors spread like wildfire. Simms supporters said that Mackey had filed charges with the attorney general accusing him of being "perniciously active" in politics while being a government employee. Mackey responded by issuing a $1,000 reward for anyone who could produce evidence that he had ever filed such a request.

"Col. Mackey knows well that he did not file any written charges, but that he did go to the department and call attention to the fact that I want running against him," Simms told the *Washington Times.* "He was told that if he had any charges to make to put them in writing."

Newspapers across the state took notice, editorializing support for the crusading prosecutor from Alexandria County.

"Crandal Mackey has cleaned out the gambling dens of Alexandria County," the *Culpepper Enterprise* reported. "He is a terror to evil-doers."

Simms didn't stand a chance. Mackey swamped him at the polls. It was such a resounding victory that Mackey briefly considered challenging Congressman C.C. Carlin, the lawyer who had represented the St. Asaph Racetrack at the beginning of his term. He had been appointed to fill the unexpired term of John Rixey, who died unexpectedly in February 1907, so 1908 would have been the best possible chance to unseat him. Carlin represented a kind of dragon to Mackey, who desperately wanted to slay the corruption that was rampant in government. Mackey decided against a campaign for Congress, but he went on the warpath anyway.

"The people of Virginia are good people, and if they knew who Carlin is, the people of Virginia will not touch Mr. Carlin," Mackey declared in a speech delivered in Herndon in April 1908. "I never knew Mr. Carlin…to stand up for the principles of my county or in any other county to stand up for the principles that the good people were fighting for."

Clearly, the past haunted the present.

"My recollections of Mr. Carlin are not pleasant," Mackey continued. "Nineteen times, they go writs of prohibition against me to prevent my enforcing the law against gambling houses, and Mr. Carlin was their attorney. It was not a political matter; it was good morals and decency in a fight for your homes, and Mr. Carlin was against the homes."

That prompted a thunderous applause from the crowd in Herndon that April evening in 1908, but it may not have meant much—Carlin went on to serve another five terms in Congress. But there were other parts of the Mackey agenda that prompted thunderous applause and that had

C.C. Carlin was Crandal Mackey's archenemy, representing the gambling interests and eventually serving the interests of the Byrd machine in Congress. *Library of Congress.*

more lasting significance. One was a national highway system, a cause he supported long before the interstate highway system was on the drawing boards. Another was the Byrd liquor law, which Mackey said "could not have been better drawn in the interest of the brewers by the brewers themselves."

Here we see a passing of the torch. Senator George Mushback created anti-gambling legislation to help the gamblers as part of the Byrd machine. Now House of Delegates Speaker Richard Evelyn Byrd was pushing a liquor law that helped the brewers. Within a few years, his son, Harry Byrd, would get himself elected to the Virginia state Senate and, ultimately, become governor and create a new machine that would become the successor to the Martin machine.

Liquor was becoming quicker at the turn of the century. Saloons were starting to sell something called "near beer," which Mackey obviously suspected of being something of a fraud. He vowed to arrest any saloonkeeper who dared to sell near beer. For the crusading prosecutor, everywhere he turned he

Harry Flood Byrd created a machine from the remains of the one established a generation before by Thomas Staples Martin. *Library of Congress.*

saw an enemy trying to close in on his territory. During one public meeting, for example, Commissioner of Revenue Curtis Graham accused "strangers" of trying to introduce "corruption and crookedness" in the county.

"Do you mean me?" Mackey inquired.

"Yes," replied Graham.

Mackey then took a swing at Graham. It was not the first time or the last time that Crandal Mackey took to personal violence to settle scores. Perhaps that was an occupational hazard of being a prosecutor in an age of unending violence. In 1910, Mackey took up the case of Robert Murphy, who was killed in a field west of Alexandria. The suspect, a tramp named Michael Nolan, claimed that Murphy assaulted him with a gun. In another case, two black men were shot to death over a game of craps, and the triggerman escaped under cover of darkness.

"Several years ago, gambling and other vices flourished, free from molestation in the county and the promoters reaped a harvest, the patrons principally being Washingtonians," the *Richmond Times Dispatch* reported in 1910. "Through the untiring efforts of Crandal Mackey, the evil was stamped out, and, it appears has again been resurrected."

Liquor selling flourished in certain sections of Alexandria. Policy was being sold in Rosslyn and Jackson City. Whiskey was flowing freely in Hell's Bottom. Evil was returning to Alexandria County. Judge J.B.T. Thornton threated to keep the grand jury in session indefinitely if necessary.

Danger was lurking everywhere, and not just for Crandal Mackey. Those around him seem to suffer as well. Just as he launched his campaign against saloons and gamblers in 1904, the Mackey family servant, Lelia Adams, was assaulted while passing over a lonely part of the road on the way home from Rock Hill, the Mackey home. Adams, a twenty-four-year-old black woman, suffered a dozen cuts on her head. When questioned by detectives, she said she knew of no reason for the assault.

A few years later, in 1911, Crandal Mackey's wife was viciously attacked at Rock Hill. She was alone in the house, bending over a basket of laundry, when a black man appeared out of the shadows. At first, she thought it was an old servant who sometimes stayed at the house. But a second look persuaded her that she was mistaken.

"How dare you come into my room!" she yelled.

The man, six feet tall and powerfully built, lunged at her, grabbing her throat and threatening to kill her. Then, suddenly, the sound of footsteps spooked the man, and he ran down the hallway. The woman grabbed a revolver and gave chase. But he was gone, just the latest in a string of violent home invasions that the *Washington Herald* dubbed "the most daring ever perpetrated in the history of the county." Every man who owned an automobile volunteered to patrol the roads.

"Not only was the attack singularly bold, committed as it was with every room in the house," the *Washington Herald* reported, "but it was planned and executed to the minutest detail."

When an organized and lawless band of criminals began terrorizing Rosslyn. Mackey went out on the warpath. This time, he left his law books behind and grabbed his shotgun instead. When a neighbor said that he saw a man acting suspiciously on a bicycle, the crusading prosecutor knew he was hot on the trail. Searching behind a feed store, Mackey found his man—a suspect who would later be identified as George Williams, described by the *Washington Herald* as "repulsive," with several scars on the side of his face.

"Throw up your hands," Mackey demanded, according to newspapers accounts. Williams was also packing heat. Apparently, the suspect had a fully loaded 0.32-caliber revolver in his hip pocket. A search of his house uncovered a watch he had stolen from a neighbor the same night as the Mackey home invasion. He told investigators that he got the scars on his face during a fight in Newberry, South Carolina, several years earlier.

But even as Mackey wrapped up one case, more acts of senseless violence kept erupting. In the summer of 1910, the *Alexandria Gazette* reported a shocking case in Hell's Bottom involving two black men accused of being accomplices in the shooting death of another black man during a dispute over a game of craps. Mackey led the prosecution against the two men—one was discharged, while the other was found guilty of gambling and carrying a concealed weapon. The triggerman escaped the night of the murder and was never prosecuted. It seemed that gambling and vice was once again flourishing in Alexandria County.

Meanwhile, a glut of cases at the courthouse involved Sheriff Palmer and Commonwealth's Attorney Mackey cracking down on vice and gambling. At the end of June, the court considered several cases of policy being played at Rosslyn and Jackson City while whiskey was being sold at Hell's Bottom, Queen City and Johnson's Hill.

"Mackey said that policy could be stopped by arresting all players for vagrancy," the *Alexandria Gazette* reported.

Much of what Mackey accomplished in his years as a prosecutor involved prosecuting African American men. In many of the cases, it was black-on-black crime—a phrase that means much more today than it did back then. While the Southern Progressive movement was driven by a desire to suppress the black vote, Mackey enjoyed a solid reputation in the African American community. A black newspaper known as the *Washington Bee* splashed his picture across the top of its front pages on February 25, 1911, as part of its plan "to give honor and credit to white men regardless of their party affiliations."

"Mr. Mackey has on more than one occasion demonstrated to the entire satisfaction of the Negro hereabouts his sincerity in demanding equal justice for all men, regardless of the color of their skin or the texture of their hair," the *Washington Bee* noted.

To underscore that point, the *Bee* reminded readers of two recent cases. One involved a young white woman who sauntered into the woods of Rosslyn with a male companion before charging that he had been shot by some unknown Negro. The case aroused a great deal of interest, and Mackey issued a statement in defense of the Negroes of his county. Washington police arrested a man, but Mackey let him go when it became clear that he had a solid alibi.

"No doubt an innocent life was saved," the *Bee* observed.

The other case cited by the *Bee* involved the murder of a white man near Four Mile Run. Four black men were arrested, one of whom turned state's evidence and concocted an elaborate confession in which the other three forced him to participate in a robbery and murder. The other three were sentenced to the hangman's gallows in Alexandria city. Feelings were so raw in the city that the three were moved to the Alexandria County jail. There, under intense questioning of Crandal Mackey, he admitted that his false confession was coerced by the Alexandria police.

"The *Bee* hopes to see the day that this highly worthy patriotic man will take his seat in Congress as the Representative from his district," the newspaper reported. "In this regard, let every colored man do his utmost to bring about this result, and thereby show the gratitude of the race for the Honorable Crandal Mackey and all other white men of the same make-up."

The Progressive League clearly agreed, handing Mackey a full-throated endorsement for a third term in 1911. The organization castigated the "small clique" of government officials who controlled county finances. The league said that large tracts of land were held by nonresident spectators, who were charged ridiculously low assessments as part of some kind of sweetheart deal. That depleted the county's funds for education, forcing the school system to close early for the summer.

That put Superintendent of Schools James Clements in the thick of things. He was one of the two Democrats challenging Mackey that year in November. A former commonwealth's attorney who was defeated for reelection in the 1890s, Clements was a mercurial real estate agent who was trying to stage a comeback. Clements announced his candidacy in May 1911 and immediately went on the attack. On the campaign trail, Clements claimed that gambling places had once again opened for business in Alexandria County and that more than fifty speakeasies were in operation.

Richard Moncure was another Democrat challenging Mackey that November. A wealthy man with many connections, Moncure had a campaign strategy very similar to the one Clements was using. Over and over again on the campaign trail, Moncure accused Mackey of being a corrupt politician who was using his power and influence to allow crime to fester unchecked. This was a departure from his support of Mackey the previous year.

"While serving in his official capacity as Commonwealth's Attorney, Mr. Mackey has done much toward the abolishment of gambling and drinking in this county," Moncure wrote in September 2, 1910. "He has been an energetic and capable official and deserves credit for the work he has done and the results obtained."

By the campaign season of 1911, Moncure had flip-flopped. Now he was out for blood, and he no longer believed that Mackey was an energetic and capable official who had done much toward the abolishment of gambling and drinking in Alexandria County. During one of the more dramatic moments in the campaign, Moncure staged a rally at the county courthouse to show moving pictures and stereopticon views of alleged gambling houses and speakeasies.

"Enthusiasm was rampant, and personalities abounded," the *Washington Times* reported. "The campaign thus far has been noted for the bitter feeling displayed on both sides."

The 1911 campaign represented somewhat of a turning point for Crandal Mackey. Aside from the violence in Georgetown, it was also a time when the commonwealth's attorney had reached a zenith of power. Mackey had become chairman of the local Democratic committee, a position that put him at the center of power in Alexandria County.

"The political campaign has been a warm one, full of accusations and personalities," the *Washington Herald* reported. "The fight between the candidates for office of commonwealth's attorney has been one of the fiercest."

The campaign took a bizarre turn one afternoon in Georgetown. Clements was eating at a place called Koester's lunchroom on M Street. Mackey supporter Amos Donaldson of Cherrydale strolled into the lunchroom. Donaldson was in the brick businesses and was a longtime Mackey supporter. He saw Clements and immediately started talking trash.

"Crandal Mackey is going to be elected again," Donaldson proclaimed.

"I think you are mistaken, Amos," the candidate responded.

"You're the little end of nothing," Donaldson shot back. "You don't count for a thing. You won't even figure in this election. It's all going Mackey's way."

They took the confrontation outside. Clements pulled a rusty 0.32-caliber revolver from his pocket and fired a shot into the air. "I only fired once, and I did that to scare him," Clements told the *Washington Times*. "It was no more than any other self respecting gentleman would have done."

When the police showed up, the candidate explained that Donaldson was a large man, and he felt he needed the revolver as protection. He was taken to the Seventh Precinct for questioning. "I had to do it to preserve my standing in the community," Clements would later tell a newspaper reporter. "Suppose I had let him beat me in the street. Could I have been elected?"

A few weeks later, Clements announced that he was suspending his campaign and endorsing Moncure. "At the urgent request of a number of my friends and recognizing the fact myself that with two candidates in the field against Crandal Mackey weakens the opposition of wither, I have agreed to withdraw," Clements said in a written statement. "I want to assure my friends that my withdrawal has resulted in disappointment to me but I thank my friends for their support, and I trust that this will be transferred to Mr. Moncure."

Mackey knew that he was in a tough spot, and he needed to respond to the many charges against him. So, he staged a massive campaign rally in Clarendon. Taking the stage, he lambasted Moncure as a "tool of the liquor and gambling element," a candidate who could not be trusted. The *Bee* told its readers that Mackey had "rendered valuable services to the colored people" and had earned their support. The Progressive League stood by its man. The *Times-Dispatch* called the campaign "the most bitter political campaign ever before waged in Alexandria County." Suspense was building as election day drew closer.

"Alexandria County is more wrought up over the coming event than it has been for years," the *Washington Times* noted. "The contest is the warmest one of the campaign."

When the polls closed at sundown, the election judges gathered to start counting and recounting the votes. Newspaper accounts reported that they stayed up all night long, checking and rechecking. It wasn't until after 5:00 a.m. the next morning that they finally announced the results—Mackey won the election with 692 votes compared to Moncure's 439 votes. Despite the bitter tone of the campaign, Mackey and Moncure made a point of sitting across the table from each other at a banquet for the Citizens' Committee of Alexandria County a few weeks after the election.

"The orchestra played in a minor strain," the *Times* reported. "A corps of waiters waited through nine courses."

With the election behind him, Mackey turned to another knock-down-drag-out fight—this one against Alexandria City Hall, which wanted to annex part of the Jefferson District. Mackey led the campaign against this, asking his old friend and former Governor Andrew Jackson Montague to join the fight. The part of Del Ray that Alexandria wanted to acquire was worth a cool $1 million. The county government paid the former governor and his brother $3,000 to work with Mackey and defeat the effort to beat Samuel Fisher, the city attorney who was leading the fight for Alexandria.

This was a time when boxcar robbers hustled their way onto the trains at Potomac Yard and hobos were caught sleeping in the hedges. Congress would regularly treat the District of Columbia as some sort of pet project, like the Tallahassee congressman who demanded an immediate ban on all gas heaters in the District, which he considered a fire hazard. Meanwhile, across the river, Alexandria City Hall was engaged in an all-out war with the Alexandria county courthouse.

"The employment of such able counsel to oppose annexation means that Alexandria is going to have a great big fight on its hands before it succeeds in acquiring any part of the territory of Alexandria County," the *Washington Herald* concluded.

At City Hall, members of the board of aldermen met and appropriated $3,000 to take on Mackey and the governor. Even before the common council approved the measure, city leaders were spoiling for a fight. The city attorney rounded up a group of "well-known attorneys." Fairfax County Commonwealth's Attorney C. Vernon Ford offered his services to the city. Each side set in for another epic court battle, this one perfectly timed for the upcoming election. "That the measure will be fought to the last inch seems certain," the *Washington Times* observed. "However, the feeling here is equally tense, and no stone will be left unturned to bring it about."

In April, the Democratic Executive Committee of Alexandria gathered at the county courthouse and appointed Mackey a delegate to the state convention. At the time, the western border of Alexandria city was Payne Street, and the northern border was Montgomery Street. Today, these are approximately the boundaries of Old Town. The proposal the city was pushing in the courts would have extended the boundary all the way to Lloyd's Lane, a first attempt at pushing into Del Ray.

Governor William Hodges Mann appointed Judge B.T. Gordon of the Twenty-ninth Judicial Circuit to handle the case. Unlike other states, where issues of annexation were decided by juries or a popular ballot, Virginia's laws provided that such proceedings would be decided by a likely disinterested judge. His decision on the matter was final and not subject to appeal, which meant that both sides had everything riding on what happened in Gordon's courtroom.

The parties gathered in May and spent the better part of a day engaged in legal arguments on both sides. But a technical point derailed the proceedings. Gordon ruled that the city erred in serving papers to members of the board of supervisors as individuals rather than as a body. The city considered the technical problem a stumbling block, but not a fatal one. They resolved to file papers again, correctly this time, leading to another trial in September— just in time for the election.

On August 7, as Mackey was preparing for the trail, disaster almost struck. While driving with his wife and two daughters on Rock Hill Road along "Dead Man's Hollow," Mackey was blinded by the lights of another automobile coming over the top of the hill and lost control of the car. The rear wheel of the automobile went over the side of the road, and the vehicle plunged over a twenty-five-foot embankment. The automobile turned completely over twice, but the fall was broken by a wire fence at the bottom of the hill. Amazingly, the Mackeys sustained no serious injury.

"The escape was miraculous," Mackey told the *Washington Times*. "I do not see how we all escaped being killed."

Despite his brush with death, the commonwealth's attorney was ready for the trial against City Hall. When city officials called Alexandria Police Chief Charles Good to the stand, they wanted him to testify that Del Ray lacked police protection that Alexandria could provide. But they may not have expected what happened next. On cross examination, the prosecutor got the police chief to admit that whiskey was served illegally in city resorts and that his officers made no arrests. The judge dismissed the suit, rejecting the city's claim that it was too congested.

Overcrowding was also at the heart of another heated case Mackey took up that year, a prosecution against the Great Falls and Old Dominion Railroad Company. Mackey brought a case against the railroad, charging that the cars were too crowded and that passengers were compelled to stand throughout long rides. He said that stations were inadequate and that no provisions were made "for the comfort of the ladies."

Tension boiled over at a meeting to discuss the grievances. Mackey launched into an opening statement, accusing the company of violating the standards of decency. Attorney John Lyon then spoke to defend the railroad, which was run by powerful men with deep pockets. The *Washington Herald* reported that it was a "warm debate spiced with epithets," culminating in a heated exchange. Mackey took a swing at Lyon, landing a right hook on his nose.

"The old courthouse has been the scene of many frays," the *Herald* reported. "With these fresh in their minds, the peace-loving citizens made a break for the door."

THE FINAL CAMPAIGN

By 1915, Crandal Mackey had become part of the machine he was elected to overturn. Or at least that's how his opponents within the Democratic Party began viewing him. As the political season began heating up that year, it became clear that the three-term prosecutor would have to fight for his job in a primary battle. His own party turned against him.

The list of serious rivals aiming to oust the forty-nine-year-old Mackey is an indication that many viewed him as weak, an incumbent that could be knocked off if the conditions were right. He had never faced so many opponents in any of his three previous races, even when the forces of corrupt politicians and gambling money were aligned against him. Considering the young ages of the challengers, the campaign must have been viewed as a sort of generational battle.

The most serious challenge came from twenty-nine-year-old Frank Livingston Ball, a native of Clarendon who hailed from one of the county's most celebrated families. He attended public schools in the county and then went across the river to Western High School in Washington, D.C. After graduating high school in 1905, Ball worked his way though the National Law School in Washington and received a bachelor of law degree in 1908.

"He has never been connected to with any ring, machine or boss," reported the *Monitor*, a progressive newspaper published by Frank Lyon in Rosslyn. "But he has been a free lance in all county fights, fighting clean hard and in the open."

A campaign photo of
Commonwealth's Attorney
Crandal Mackey in 1915. *Virginia
Room, Arlington Public Library.*

In Ball's short political career, he could already count one major political triumph. Back in 1911, he beat a candidate with heavy machine backing for a spot on the Democratic Committee in 1911. Now he hoped to pull off another political miracle, beating the powerful commonwealth's attorney. If he won, he would be the youngest prosecutor ever elected in the county.

Even at his young age, Ball was already earning the nickname "the Wizard" for the spell he cast over juries, a talent that has clear advantages on the campaign trail. Ball's own father had personally selected Mackey to challenge the previous commonwealth's attorney, so the decision to take on the incumbent is an indication of how dramatically the political environment had changed in the past twelve years.

Ball was not alone. Other challengers included thirty-six-year-old Charles Thomas Jesse of Fort Myer Heights, a native of Carolina County who spent several years building a legal career in New York City before returning to the commonwealth and establishing himself as a leader in the Bar Association of the Sixteenth Judicial Circuit. Then there was thirty-six-year-old Judge Robert Gordon Finney of Clarendon, a native of Powhatan County who resigned his position as a trial justice to campaign for commonwealth's attorney.

In a bold letter to the *Monitor*, Mackey unleashed a prosecution of his opponents with the same fury he went after gamblers and liquor sellers. As a prosecutor who shut down the gambling houses and undermined the political machine, Mackey threw the gauntlet down. Clearly, he was ready to scrap for a fourth term.

"I have more enemies than any man in the county with the possible exception of my friend Frank Lyon," he wrote, referring to the muckraking newspaperman of Rosslyn.

Lyon's newspaper, the *Monitor*, would play a critical role in the election of 1915. Mackey wrote a long letter to the editor, which was published on the front page along with a campaign photo of the commonwealth's attorney. It began with the familiar narrative of that fateful meeting at the home of William Ball. He recalled waiting along with the other candidates in the darkened stable behind the house, a tense moment that would have drastic consequences for Mackey and for Alexandria County. In a moment of self-deprecating humor, he observed that the only reason they had selected him is that he "looked healthy."

"Vice and crime were rampant and firmly entrenched here," he wrote. "The county was covered with gambling houses and Sunday bars. Every variety of crime including murder went unpunished. The black banners of official corruption floated over the county."

Framing his story as a classic David versus Goliath, Mackey said that "all the powers of political organization and unlimited money" were used to defeat him. Once again, Mackey told the story of how he was elected with a two-vote margin of victory. And he recounted how a team of nine lawyers charged that money had been used to secure the election of 1903, an allegation he said could be made only "with grim irony and an irresistible sense of humor."

Within a few months, the candidate explained, he had closed every gambling house and Sunday bar in Alexandria County. He praised the "upright judge" and "manly men" that stood at his back, describing his early years in office as a harrowing ordeal.

"Looking back through the twists of years to those days of lawlessness and corruption, days of threats, menace, intimidation, insult and exhortation, days of worry and discouragement and sleepless nights and hopeless appeals to the state government for protection," he wrote, "I wonder myself how the great task of cleaning up the county was accomplished."

Mackey had become nostalgic for the bad old days. He described the "sweetest memories" of that era as "tender and intimate," yet he made it clear that he was not willing to exit the public stage anytime soon. After all these years of fighting for Alexandria County, he said, was it so strange that he was not willing to step down? For his part, he made it clear that he was not about to watch as three young men engaged in a scramble for his office.

One by one, he addressed his opponents. George Chadwick was dismissed as someone who needed the money. As for Frank Ball and Robert Gordon Finney and Charles Thomas Jesse, he didn't think that they were cut out for the job—at least not yet. They were "capable young lawyers of clean life and high characters." Turning his fire directly on his chief opponent and former protégé, Mackey mercilessly ridiculed Ball's campaign promise to conduct the county's business at the courthouse.

"It is hard to imagine where else he could attend to county business," Mackey observed. "He might have added that if elected he would be willing to die at the courthouse."

Here Mackey's sense of humor emerges from the dusty old newspaper copy. He wrote that Ball could have well said that he will try all cases at the circuit court at the courthouse, meet the board of supervisors at the courthouse, visit the clerk's office at the courthouse, draw his salary at the courthouse and eat his lunch at the courthouse. And then he sharpened the knife, implying that Ball's power relied on nepotism: "Certainly all family reunions could be appropriately held at the courthouse."

Ball's stump speech invariably focused attention on his long history in the county, reminding voters that he was born and raised in Alexandria County. Mackey, on the other hand, was born in a Confederate ambulance down in Louisiana. That's not exactly the kind of local connection that grabs the attention of constituents. Mackey wanted to make the most of his situation and undercut the strength of his opponent, so he explained that Ball reminded him of the man who applied for the position of sexton for a church and, when asked for his qualifications, replied that his grandfather had been pallbearer at George Washington's funeral.

"I unfortunately had no choice as to the place of my birth," Mackey explained. "My parents were not in a position to consult me and my mother had troubles of her own at the time, but knowing the conditions in Alexandria County when Mr. Ball was born I think there would have been no picnic ants on my judgment if I had chosen to be ushered into the world in some other jurisdiction."

Mackey reminded readers that he had twelve years of drawing indictments, twelve years of prosecutions and twelve years of attending to the county's civil business. During those dozen years, he said, the municipality had never lost a case.

"I have never used the powers of my office to oppress even the humblest negro, nor asked for unreasonable punishment or demanded excessive bail," Mackey boasted. "No doubt my opponents will say that I am entitled to no credit for this because my head is shaped that way and I can't help it."

Aside from shutting down the saloons and gambling halls, Mackey said that another part of his legacy was fighting encroachment from city officials in Alexandria. During an annexation case, for example, Mackey reminded readers that Alexandria tried to take about $1 million worth of land. The city lost that case in circuit court, Mackey reminded readers, and got less than it asked for on final hearing in the court of appeals.

And then there was the case involving the superintendent of schools who had been paid $1,800 illegally. That case had been argued and submitted to the jury, although a decision in the case was still pending at the time. Mackey also acquired more than fifty rights-of-way along Mount Vernon Avenue—a part of Alexandria County that would become the town of Potomac and, ultimately, the Del Ray neighborhood. Even more recently, he had been working to secure rights-of-way for the new Russell Road, which was intended to shorten the travel time between Washington and Alexandria. "The matters with the growing civil business of the county have been so burdensome and taken up so much of my time that I have only recently determined to run again for office," the prosecutor explained.

Mackey also presented himself as a grass-roots politician who believed that citizens associations suggested the best measures to the Alexandria County Board of Supervisors. During the most recent session of the General Assembly, he had lobbied for a proposal to abolish the fee system in which payments could be made directly to justices of the peace, sheriffs, constables, witnesses and clerks. Instead, Mackey argued, the officials should receive a salary.

"The wand of law and order has been passed over the county and villages like exhalations have arising from the ground," Mackey proclaimed. "However small the office of commonwealth's attorney may be in the other ninety-nine counties of Virginia, in Alexandria County, situated opposite Washington, the OFFICE IS A MAN'S JOB."

Were Mackey's opponents men? He does not offer an answer, but the implication is clear. Mackey clearly thought that he was the man for the job. Not everyone agreed. Lyon's newspaper, the *Monitor*, endorsed Charles Thomas Jesse for the job. It was a rebuke to the iconoclastic commonwealth's attorney who had once been the darling of the progressive movement. In the eyes of Lyon and other progressives in the county, Mackey had become a part of the same machine he once raged against.

"Here is a candidate to suit the quiet, orderly people of the county who would like to see the law dealt out equally to the strong and the weak alike," the *Monitor* editorialized. "He has the united opposition of what for a better term is designated as the courthouse crowd. They will support Crandal Mackey to a man."

Railing against the courthouse crowd, the *Monitor* castigated what it called "the sporting fraternity" as a crowd of insiders. Members of the newspaper's editorial board liked the fact that Jesse was a newcomer, untainted by the inner circle of power. They liked the fact that he wasn't born in Alexandria and that his parents weren't born in Alexandria—an implicit rebuke to Frank Ball.

"Mr. Jesse is no orator in the ordinary acceptance of that word," the paper editorialized. "However he has one of the great if not the greatest essential of oratory—sincerity."

The *Monitor* suggested that some men might be able to hold the interest of the public without sincerity. But in the end, the paper wrote, insincerity will unmask the guilty culprit. And then he will cease to move the crowd. Although the paper did not specifically call out Mackey, why else would this explanation appear as a reason to dump an incumbent? Clearly, the muckraking progressive newspaper of record in Rosslyn had turned its back on Mackey. Members of the editorial board believed that no change could be expected at the courthouse by returning the same crowd to power.

"It is fully understood that many people in the county approve of conditions as they exist at the courthouse and these people will vote for a continuance in office of our quadrennial candidates who have been responsible for existing conditions," the paper editorialized. "This editorial is addressed to those who believe there should be a change."

Jesse would be free to act, the editorial suggested, because the courthouse gang had always opposed him. The *Monitor* described the Mackey administration as a kind of unthinking machine that was willing to demolish anything or anybody in its way. As far as the other candidates were concerned, the *Monitor* believed that Frank Ball represented a style of nepotistic insider politics that had become a problem in Alexandria County.

"He is not tied to any of the officeholders by ties of blood that so often embarrass in the performance of official duty," the *Monitor* explained. "He would not stand for making his office a public nuisance for the enforcement of blue laws in Virginia."

Ever since seventeenth-century New Haven colonists had printed laws designed to regulate moral behavior on blue paper, the mandates have been known as "blue laws." Traditionally, the phase is used to describe legislation designed to enforce religious standards, particularly the observance of Sunday as a day of worship and rest. Many are still on the books today, including a section of the Virginia code that notes that traditional forms of hunting on Sunday are illegal, except for raccoons.

The *Monitor*'s editorialists clearly believed that Mackey's righteous crusade against Sunday bars had become an embarrassment, drawing attention to Alexandria County as a land of sanctimonious holy rollers. Jesse came from New York City, a place where blue laws were viewed as some sort of backwater defect. There, along the alleys of the Bowery, he learned that dancing and theaters are not immoral.

Perhaps even more important was this: if people wanted to buy tobacco or newspapers on a Sunday, more power to them. The vast majority of the people wanted the government to stay out of their lives on Sunday, easing restrictions on commerce and modern life.

In the end, the *Monitor* concluded, Mackey had simply been in office too long. Rotation in office was the only way to ensure clean government, untainted by the corrupting influence of power. The newspaper figured that it didn't matter much what the candidates had to say about what they would do if elected. Instead, the editorial warned, only their public record could explain who these men were and what they were up to.

"The power of the office is so great that it should remain in the hands of no one man for over two terms," the *Monitor* concluded. "He gets to be in the very nature of things too much of an autocrat."

As October began, the campaign was in full swing. With just a month before election day, the race had become a referendum on Crandal Mackey, blue laws, morality, alcohol, nepotism and autocracy. During an October 8 rally at Ballston, all of the candidates for office appeared and presented themselves to voters. Candidates for various offices spoke to voters and made their closing case heading into election day.

As it turns out, the Ballston rally would become an important moment in the campaign, although it was not clear at first how much. The first stir of the day was created by A.C. Clements, a candidate for sheriff. He told voters that someone told the Civil Service Commission that he was running for office, and he ended up losing his job. "This created quite a sensation," the newspaper reported, "and produced much sympathy."

That wasn't the only sensation of the day. The real draw for the rally was the hotly contested campaign for commonwealth's attorney. When the time came, it seemed as though something was missing, or perhaps someone. All three of his challengers were there waiting for their turn, but Crandal Mackey was nowhere to be found. "The audience craned their necks looking for him to appear but it was in vain," the *Monitor* reported.

Ball, who had emerged as the frontrunner in the race, spoke first. He recalled his life in the county and his attendance at local schools. Here was a man truly in his element at Ballston, which had originally been known as Ball's crossroads because of the tavern his family once operated there. The candidate outlined his intention to have an office at the courthouse, promising that, if elected, he would strictly enforce the law.

"He made an excellent impression and seemed to have the audience with him," the *Monitor* noticed. "Mr. Ball is extremely popular not only in this section but through the county and the audience showed its approval."

Robert Gordon Finney then took the stage to blast Mackey for running a political machine at the courthouse. The candidate said that everything at the courthouse was dominated by one interest and that Mackey had become "part and parcel of the organization." Finney raised a rally in Ballston four years ago in which Mackey abruptly switched his endorsement regarding which candidate he would be supporting for clerk of court.

Finally, it was Charles Jesse's turn. The candidate told the crowd that the subject of his address would be "the system." By that, he meant the courthouse organization that controlled all the finances of the county, private and public as well as offices. Turning his attention to Mackey, Jesse said that the best evidence that the incumbent was corrupt was his support from Rosslyn Milling Company owner A.D. Torreyson, as well as notorious businessman George Rucker.

"It was an interesting meeting. The audience was equal in intelligence and character of any that has ever assembled in Virginia," the *Monitor* reported. "If they vote for crooks, it will be a deliberate vote."

But Mackey was back at it a few days later in Clarendon. According to a report in the *Washington Herald*, Mackey spoke "at length" on the reasons why his twelve years in office had "eminently fitted him to continue the work."

But then something happened. Two days after the Clarendon speech, Mackey appeared for a meeting of voters in Cherrydale. Unexpectedly, and without much explanation, he dropped out of the race. It would be a surprising swan song for the prosecutor, signaling an end to his days as an elected official. Nobody knew why, or at least they weren't saying anything if they did.

"His action was a complete surprise," the *Herald* reported. "He told the Cherrydale voters last night that work he started when he took office twelve years ago had been finished and declared that the gambling, illegal sale of liquor, and other vices rampant in the county twelve years ago practically have disappeared. He also said his law practice in Washington keeps him busy."

That didn't add up. Why would Mackey launch a campaign, write an extended defense of his career in the *Monitor* and withstand the criticism of his detractors if he felt his job had already been accomplished? Why would Mackey choose to make this momentous decision less than a month from election day? Why would he mix it up with his competitors only to conclude that any of them would be qualified to succeed him?

Unfortunately, we are left without answers. "Mr. Mackey recommended to the voters any one of the three men seeking the Commonwealth's attorneyship—Frank Ball, Charles Jesse or Gordon Finney," the *Herald* reported.

The next few days were a flurry of campaigning, with the remaining candidates working feverishly to fill the void left by the longtime incumbent. "Since the withdrawal of the Commonwealth's Attorney Mackey from the race, all three candidates have been out in force soliciting votes," the *Herald* reported.

Mackey's exit from the race raised an important question in the county's political circles: which candidate would "the organization" support? That was the question posed by the *Monitor*, which defined "the organization" as "that small coterie of county officials and their favorites who have filled the offices generally of the county for the last generation."

At this point, the *Monitor* revealed the subtle racism at work in the politics of the era. The newspaper castigated the political machine at the county courthouse as controlling the vote of "the negro, the gambler, the saloon and those who eat crumbs that fall from the table of the mighty." Support from the machine was an asset and a liability, with strong partisans eager to line up on either side of power.

"Ugly rumors are in the air," the *Monitor* declared ominously. "The organization had better be circumspect and cover its tracks because the other two candidates might find it advisable to combine and cast a solid vote against the organization."

On election day, all the saloons and banks were closed, preventing people from getting too drunk or too rich. The polls were open from 6:27 a.m. (sunrise) to 5:00 p.m. Virginia Senator Richard Ewell Thornton and Delegate John Fred Birrell were running unopposed, which meant that the race for commonwealth's attorney was at the top of the ticket.

Also on the ballot that day were two candidates for the Jefferson District of the Arlington County Board of Supervisors, four candidates for the Arlington District, two candidates for the Washington District, five candidates for sheriff, two candidates for commissioner of revenue, three candidates for treasurer, three candidates for overseer of the poor, twelve candidates for constable and fourteen candidates for justice of the peace.

"The election in the county promises to be exciting," the *Washington Times* reported. "The withdrawal of Crandal Mackey from the race complicated matters to some extent."

Ball won in a landslide with 931 votes, or 68 percent of the voters. Finney captured 23 percent of the vote with 319. Jesse finished last with 118, or 9 percent of the electorate.

Almost immediately after the election, the view of Crandal Mackey moved from machine politician to revered public official. The *Monitor* editorialized that Alexandria County was losing "an efficient public servant." The same newspaper that had only recently described him as leading a "sporting fraternity" of insiders had now decided that he was a figure of historic importance.

"He took over the affairs of the commonwealth's attorney's office when this county was overrun with gamblers and illicit liquor sellers," the *Monitor* editorialized. "Gambling dens were at every entrance to the county and thousands from Washington came over every Sunday to debauch in Virginia and bring disgrace to our borders."

Here was the newspaper that endorsed Charles Thomas Jesse, who received 9 percent of the vote, describing Rosslyn, Jackson City and St. Asaph as "pest holes" where "murder and rapine were everywhere." All that was now "but a memory" for county residents, many of whom had moved there since the change and had no idea what a sorry state of affairs had prevailed.

"The history of the expulsion of these dens from among us is the proudest page in the traditions of our county, and Capt. Mackey is the man who led the fight and worsted the enemies of decent government," the *Monitor* noted. "From the day he stepped into office they were doomed."

Within a few months of Mackey's inauguration, the paper explained, their operations were shut down, never to reopen. The evil influences that "robbed the citizens of this county of their right to a quiet and peaceful existence" had been "forever silenced."

Ultimately, Crandal Mackey threw open the doors to the Progressive era of Alexandria County.

"The best wishes of our county go with Capt. Mackey and those who have been here longest and know best what a good work he was wrought will forever feel grateful to him," the *Monitor* reported. "He retires from office with a clean slate and with the knowledge of duty well done, and, after all, this is the greatest reward."

Meanwhile, the *Monitor* seemed even more excited about Ball: "He believed that the government belongs to the people and is always ready and willing to get every public questions properly in the hands of the great mass of people for settlement."

THE REST OF THE STORY

When it was all over, supporters gathered at the Del Ray schoolhouse to celebrate the life and times of Crandal Mackey. The school, which was located on the site of the modern-day Mount Vernon Community School, was a valedictory of sorts. Gathered in the chilly schoolhouse that January evening, friends and former enemies gathered to observe the end of an era. Crandal Mackey was leaving the corner office at the Alexandria County Courthouse. But he wasn't leaving without making his mark.

"If the good he succeeds in accomplishing is to be permanent, he must be supported by a determined public sentiment," the *Washington Times* noted. "The people must approve his action and stand steadfast in opposition to vice and crime."

Former Alexandria Mayor George Simpson spoke first, praising the "public morals" of the "zealous prosecuting officer." Reprising a joke that was used when Mackey was victorious over the racetrack, one speaker said the prosecutor would be able to give a lecture on the best method of "making a graft on a plum tree." Alexandria County *Monitor* Editor Frank Lyon said that the people had chosen Mackey because they had confidence that he would do everything in mortal power to make gambling a thing of the past.

"It is due to Mr. Mackey's energy and devotion to duty that Fort Myer is not surrounded by the low and degrading influences which characterize the environment of so many army posts, and that railway men and employees of the brickyard and other industries are not subjected to the temptations afforded by low saloons and gambling resorts," the *Washington Herald* noted.

Looking down the barrel of Crandal Mackey's infamous shotgun. *Brandy Crist-Travers.*

The torch had been passed to a new generation. That was perhaps most evident in Jackson City, where it was more than just passed to the next generation—it was handed to an arsonist. A few years after Mackey left office, a gambler by the name of John Nelson was on a barstool in a saloon across from the Bureau of Engraving and Printing. Inexplicably, he started bragging to other patrons about how he was going to write the final chapter in the long and sordid history of Jackson City.

"I'm going over and burn that place down," he said, according to one account. "You just wait right here. I'll be back in a few minutes. Just look over there, and you'll see the fire and I'll come back here and tell you what I did."

With that, Nelson took a swig of whiskey and headed to Jackson City. Before he returned, patrons at the bar could see smoke across the river. Soon afterward, Nelson arrived on his horse. He strolled into Amans Saloon and declared victory. "Boys, I told you what I was going to do, didn't I? Look over there, she's a goner this time," he exclaimed. "I fixed her this time."

Arson is a serious crime in Virginia, and Nelson had to face the music eventually. He got the best lawyer in Northern Virginia, and the trial became a pubic spectacle. Defense attorney Walton Moore made a nuanced argument to the jury. "Gentlemen of the jury. John said he didn't burn the city down. He says he didn't do it," Moore said. "But I want to say something to you about it. If he did burn it down, it is the greatest favor ever done to Arlington County by any human being."

The jury deliberated for about five minutes, returning with an acquittal. Jackson City disappeared forever.

The legacy of Crandal Mackey is more than what was accomplished during his twelve years in office. It was what was lost forever. Ask people today about Jackson City, and one is confronted with a skeptical glance. Start talking about the St. Asaph Racetrack, and one is likely to meet a wall of blank faces. Don't bother trying to explain the hidden history of Rosslyn—about crime and corruption and graft and greed—to the lunchtime crowd that gathers everyday in Crandal Mackey Park. They don't want to hear it.

Time has moved on. The same could be said for Crandal Mackey after he left office at the age of fifty. He had given the best years of his life to the fight, and now it was time to move on to something else. He wrote a history of Alexandria County. He edited a local weekly newspaper called the *Chronicle*. Ultimately, he became director of the Arlington National Bank in Rosslyn. But he was not always successful.

In 1930, he ran for Congress. At the age of sixty-six, Mackey faced serious competition in the Democratic primary. Leading the competition was forty-seven-year-old Judge Howard Smith, who was born in Fauquier County but had been practicing law in Alexandria since 1905. Then there was Mackey's old nemesis, Virginia Senator Frank Ball, who was now forty-four. Rounding out the ticket were a fifty-seven-year-old lawyer from Fairfax, Thomas Keith, and a fifty-one-year-old lawyer from Orange, Elliot Dejarnette.

Several of the candidates tried to make the perpetuation of prohibition a central focus of the campaign. But it was clear that voters had grown weary of the issue. That helped Smith, who tried to distance himself from the issue. The judge emerged as the frontrunner early in the race, with most of the newspapers endorsing his candidacy.

"While his opponents have dragged the question of prohibition into the present political contest and criticized him long and loudly for not doing the same, nevertheless it appears that he is the first of the five candidates to answer promptly and courteously but firmly the questionnaire of the Anti-Saloon League," the *Alexandria Gazette* reported. "Judge Smith states in his reply that he will not pledge himself blindfolded to any unknown legislation; to any person; at any time; on any measure."

Crandal Mackey Park is located on Nineteenth Street North between North Moore Street and North Lynn Street. *Brandy Crist-Travers.*

Smith's popularity was a testament to the changing nature of the political realm. The crusading nature of Crandal Mackey's rise to prominence was now a relic, an old trick that was no longer working. The economic collapse in 1929 transformed the political sphere.

"The Great Depression changed the character of the prohibition debate. The county desperately needed jobs. Organized labor was drumming for beer," wrote historian Garrett Peck. "A seismic shift took place in 1930 and 1932 because of the Depression, repudiating Republican policies that hadn't saved the economy."

Smith won handily in the August primary, and Mackey placed a distant fourth. But he didn't give up. Later that year, he became involved in a campaign to oppose the county manager form of government, which was on the ballot. He used the pages of the *Chronicle* to blast the plan. One headline read, "Dangerous Plan to Fasten on the County," which was accompanied by a half-page editorial outlining objections to the proposal. But the plan had powerful supporters, including Virginia Senator Frank Ball and delegate Charles Thomas Jesse—two former rivals who now formed the Arlington delegation to Richmond.

"With the opponents of the plan becoming as outspoken as those advocating it, it became obvious that a whirlwind fight on the proposed change would be staged during the remaining few days leading up to the election," wrote Robert Nelson Anderson. "Barrages from the Chronicle and the Voters Service Club continued."

But it was to no avail. In the end, the vote was 2:1 in favor of changing the form of government—2,072 for and 1,030 against.

Crandal Mackey's era was over. His popularity with voters had diminished. He was now a washed-up has-been, an elderly man with a storied past in an era looking toward the future. But in the end, the legacy of Crandal Mackey can be found in the very nature of his obscurity. The reason we don't remember his accomplishments is because the world he helped destroy has been cast into anonymity. Nowhere is this more ironic than Rosslyn, where violence and lawlessness were once commonplace. Now the neighborhood is dominated by sterile and impersonal concrete walls—a place without a sense of past. As a result, the notorious nature of its past is now taking on a new life.

"It tends to be celebrated rather than shrunk from," said Jennifer Zeien, president of the North Rosslyn Civic Association. "It's the only history Rosslyn has, and everything here dates to the 1960s. So this kind of gives it some color."

These days, Mackey has also been cast into obscurity. Few people have ever heard his name or know anything about his crusade. Part of that has

Crandal Mackey in later years.
Virginia Room, Arlington Public Library.

to do with the dramatic changes that happened in the Great Depression and World War II, which transformed Northern Virginia by flooding it with government workers.

"The Arlington and the Northern Virginia that existed before Franklin Roosevelt is lost to history," said Arlington County Board member Chris Zimmerman. "It's almost a prehistory."

Nevertheless, Mackey holds somewhat of a cult status among prosecutors. Although they may not want to admit it publically, many prosecutors have probably daydreamed about grabbing a shotgun and taking justice into their own hands. As a result, Mackey's cult status in Northern Virginia is carefully guarded, even in obscurity.

"I remember going up to the sheriff's office and seeing the shotgun mounted on the wall, and I said that shotgun belongs in the commonwealth's attorney's office," said longtime Commonwealth's Attorney Richard Trodden. "But they never would give it to me."

"It's ours," responded Arlington Sheriff Beth Arthur. "And we're keeping it."

BIBLIOGRAPHY

Alexandria Gazette. "Arrest of Gamblers." July 20, 1903.

————. "Judge Smith Given 4,848 Plurality In Eighth District." August 6, 1930.

————. "The Manager Form Carries in Arlington." November 5, 1930.

————. "Will Make Fight on Annexation." January 8, 1912.

————. "Wires Cut Out." May 20, 1904.

Anderson, Robert Nelson. *Arlington Historical Magazine*, 1958.

Ball, Frank. "The Arlington I Have Known." *Arlington Historical Magazine*, 1964.

Behrens, Steve. "Clapboard Casinos Vexed Arlington." *Northern Virginia Journal*, December 12, 1974.

Cash, W.J. *The Mind of the South.* New York: Vintage Books, 1991.

Davis, Harold. *The Americans in History.* New York: Ronald Press Company, 1953.

Dubofsky, Melvyn. *Industrialism and the American Worker, 1865–1920.* Arlington Heights, IL: Harlan Davidson, 1985.

Foster, Jack Hamilton. "Crandal Mackey, Crusading Commonwealth's Attorney." *Arlington Historical Magazine*, 1958.

Lait, Jack, and Lee Mortimer. *Washington Confidential.* New York: Crown Publishers, 1951.

Mackey, Crandal. *Brief History of Alexandria County, Virginia.* Falls Church, Virginia: Newell Printing Company, Falls Church, 1907.

Miller, T. Michael. *Alexandria (Virginia) City Officialdom 1749–1992.* Bowie, MD: Heritage Books, 1992.

Moger, Allen. *Virginia: Bourbonism to Byrd, 1870–1925.* Charlottesville: University Press of Virginia, 1968.

Monitor of Alexandria County. "Big Rally at Ballston." October 8, 1915.

————. "Charles Jesse for Commonwealth's Attorney." October 8, 1915.

————. "Commonwealth's Attorney." October 29, 1915.

————. "Mackey Announces His Candidacy for Office." September 10, 1915.

————. "New Commonwealth's Attorney Enters Office." January 7, 1916.

Montague, Ludwell Lee. *Historic Arlington.* Arlington County Historical Committee. Arlington, Virginia. 1968.

Nethernton, Nan, and Ross Nethernton. *Arlington County in Virginia: A Pictorial History.* Norfolk, VA: Donning's Company, 1987.

Northern Virginia Sun. "How Crandal Mackey Got Job to Clean Up No. Va. Gambling." April 17, 1957.

Peck, Garrett. *Prohibtion in Washington, D.C.: How Dry We Weren't.* Charleston, SC: The History Press, Charleston, 2011.

Pratt, Sherman. *Arlington County Virginia: A Modern History.* N.p., 1977.

Readnour, Harry Warren. *General Fitzhugh Lee, 1835–1905: A Biographical Study.* Charlottesville: University Press of Virginia, 1971.

Richmond Dispatch. "Andrew Jackson Montague to be Virginia's Next Governor." August 15, 1901.

————. "Clans are Gathering: Politicians and Delegates En Route for Norfolk Convention." August 13, 1901.

Richmond Times. "Advance Guard Reach Norfolk." August 13, 1901.

————. "All Ready for the Big Convention." August 11, 1901.

Richmond Times Dispatch. "Atrocious Crime in Alexandria." September 30, 1907.

————. "Fists are Used in County Meeting." May 27, 1908.

————. "Will Investigate Illegal Traffic." June 25, 1910.

Rose, Cornelia. *Arlington County, Virginia: A History.* Baltimore, MD: Port City Press, 1976.

Salmon, Emily, and Edward Campbell Jr., eds. *The Hornbook of Virginia History.* Richmond: Library of Virginia, 1994.

Templeman, Eleanor Lee. *Arlington Heritage: Vignettes of a Virginia County.* N.p.: privately self-published, 1959.

————. "Col. Mackey Closed 'Monte Carlo.'" *Northern Virginia Sun*, August 30, 1958.

————. "From Dream to Nightmare." *Northern Virginia Sun*, August 23, 1957.

Wallenstein, Peter. *Cradle of America: Four Centuries of Virginia History.* Lawrence: University Press of Kansas, 2007.

Washington Bee. "Hon. Crandal Mackey, Man of the People and Advocate of Fair Play." February 25, 1911.

Washington Herald. "Citizens Revolt Against Misrule at County Seat." August 11, 1911.

———. "County Attorney Resents the Lie with a Wallop." August 27, 1912.

———. "Crandal Mackey Out for Congress." December 6, 1911.

———. "Crandal Mackey Out of Race for Votes." October 15, 1915.

———. "Gambling Element Planning to Regain Control." March 10, 1907.

———. "Look For Quiet Election Day." November 2, 1915.

———. "Moncure a 'Liquor Tool.'" October 29, 1911.

———. "Posse in Autos Seeks Assailant of Mrs. Mackey." May 5, 1911.

———. "Prowler Caught at Point of Pistol by Mackey." May 6, 1911.

———. "Supervisors Retain Lawyers to Fight Annexation." January 3, 1912.

———. "Will Fight Mackey." December 30, 1906.

Washington Post. "Find Cache in Sewer." June 8, 1917.

———. "Have Hopes of Horse Show." August 5, 1907.

———. "Jackson City Discussed." February 11, 1892.

———. "May Lease St. Asaph's." May 24, 1917.

———. "Mayor Paff Criticizes State's Attorney Brent's St. Asaph Raid." January 19, 1905.

———. "Monte Carlo Moved." September 29, 1890.

———. "Monte Carlo Saved." October 2, 1890.

———. "Old St. Asaph Grand Stand Burns." April 19, 1916.

———. "Pipings and Clickings: Frogs Vie with the Telegraph Instruments at Jackson City." April 22, 1891.

———. "Races At St. Asaph." October 14, 1894.

———. "Racing at St. Asaph." March 16, 1894.

———. "St. Asaph Is Raided." January 10, 1905.

———. "St. Asaph Race Track Improvement." March 21, 1894.

———. "Two Fires, One Incendiary." November 2, 1914.

Washington Star. "The Old St. Asaph's Race Track Has Gone Way of All Horseflesh." February 5, 1959.

———. "On the Cloth of Green: The Minature Monte Carlo on the Other Side of the River." January 20, 1892.

Washington Times. "After Poolroom at St. Asaph." May 1, 1904.

———. "Alexandria County Election Tuesday." October 30, 1915.

———. "Attorney Mackey Must Act." September 23, 1904.

———. "Clements Quits in Alexandria Fight." November 4, 1911.

———. "Declares War Against Virginia Monte Carlo." April 24, 1904.

———. "First Gun Fired in Alexandria Annexation Fight." January 12, 1912.

———. "Flag Few High, but Nothin' Doin.'" June 14, 1904.

———. "Hiding Behind Legal Quibbles." June 30, 1904.

———. "Husband's Body Found in a Pickling Vat." July 29, 1903.

———. "Insurgency Wave Hits Alexandria." August 31, 1911.

———. "Lawyer Questions the Right of Occupation." June 10, 1903.

———. "Lid is on Tight, Says Mr. Mackey." October 29, 1908.

———. "Owners of St. Asaph Acquitted of Charges." September 17, 1904.

———. "Poolroom at St. Asaph Promises to Move Away." January 11, 1905.

———. "Poolroom Owners Now Face Arrest." September 14, 1904.

———. "Prepare Scaffold for the Hanging of John Wright." November 13, 1906.

———. "R.G. Finney Out For Mackey's Job." February 1, 1915.

———. "Simms Announces He is a Candidate." September 30, 1907.

———. "Starts Vice Crusade on All Conduit Road Sunday Lawlessness." July 13, 1906.

———. "St. Asaph Open Up for Great Suburban." June 16, 1904.

———. "St. Asaph Raid Called a Fake." January 10, 1905.

———. "Sunday Blue-Law Spasm in Rosslyn." August 18, 1902.

———. "Virginian Fires at Political Foe in Georgetown." September 22, 1911.

———. "Warrant Served Upon J.M. Hill." September 28, 1904.

Wilkinson, J. Harvie, III. *Harry Byrd and the Changing Face of Virginia Politics, 1945–1966.* Charlottesville: University Press of Virginia, 1968.

Woodward, C. Vann. "The Strange Career of Jim Crow." Oxford University Press, 1955.

INDEX

About the Author

Michael Lee Pope is an award-winning journalist who lives in Old Town Alexandria. He has reported for the *Alexandria Gazette Packet*, WAMU 88.5 News, the *New York Daily News* and the *Tallahassee Democrat*. A native of Moultrie, Georgia, he grew up in Durham, North Carolina, and graduated from high school in Tampa, Florida. He has a master's degree in American Studies from Florida State University, and he lives in the Yates Gardens neighborhood with his lovely wife, Hope Nelson.

Visit us at
www.historypress.net